To
Amy
Thanks for the support
Leeandrew Wright
9/18/16

# CRITICAL
# GRACE

## LIVING ON GOD'S LIFE SUPPORT

### PASTOR
### LEEANDREW
### WRIGHT

outskirts
press

Outskirts Press, Inc.
http://www.outskirtspress.com

Paperback ISBN: 978-1-4327-9950-2
Hardback ISBN: 978-1-4787-6756-5

Library of Congress Control Number: 2016906521

Outskirts Press and the "OP" logo are trademarks belonging to Outskirts Press, Inc.

PRINTED IN THE UNITED STATES OF AMERICA

# THIS BOOK IS DEDICATED TO THE MEMORY OF:

This book is dedicated to the memory of my parents, the late LeeAndrew Wright Sr. and Dorothene Bing. My grandparents, the late Levi and Justine Wright and William and Eunice Bing.

I would also like to dedicate this book to those who have transitioned and left an incredible legacy of laughter, love and memories. May you rest in the care of the Almighty, until that great day when you and I will meet again.

William Bing Jr., Denise Bing-Telfair, Sheryl Bing-Gladden, Mark Bing, Jaime Bing, Marolyn Wright, Willie Wright, Ernest Wright, Robert Wright, Tyrone Barrett, Chiffon Barrett, Charlie and Margaret Dickson, Timothy Bell, William Ashley, Antoine Sterling Hill, Andrae Ballard, David Wood Sr., Shron McWhorter, and Michael Williams.

To all of my ancestors who paved the way and laid the foundation, I too, will see you in the rapture.

"For the Lord Himself shall descend from heaven with a shout, with the voice of the archangel, and with the trump of God: and the dead in Christ shall rise first:

Then we which are alive and remain shall be caught up together with them in the clouds, to meet the Lord in the air: and so shall we ever be with the Lord.

Wherefore comfort one another with these words." 1 Thessalonians 4:16-18.

# AUTHOR ACKNOWLEDGMENTS:

I would like to take this time to thank some very special people in my life. I appreciate you for being a part of my journey.

I would first like to thank God, the Father – The Almighty, for allowing me the opportunity to write this devotional book. I want to thank Him for giving me the wisdom and knowledge as-well-as the patience to hear from Him and write down His heart. Thank you Father, for the gift of Salvation, for the gift of the Holy Spirit and for giving me favor!

This book was inspired by the Holy Spirit. The purpose of this book is to encourage the believer to hold on to God as they go through some of the toughest times that life will bring their way. Not only does the Lord want you to hold on, He also expects you to make it. Jeremiah 29:11 declares: "For I know the thoughts that I think toward you, saith the Lord, thoughts of peace, and not of evil, to give you and expected end."

I want to thank God for my mom and dad the late LeeAndrew Wright Sr. and Dorothene Bing. I miss you both so terribly. There isn't a day that goes by that you aren't in my thoughts, my smile, my laugh. Everything I do reminds me of the two of you. I wish you were here to share my success and to see the baby that was born so many years ago turn into a respectable young man who God is using to change lives one soul at a time.

If I could have chosen a different set of people to introduce me to this world, I'd still choose you. You are the sun in my shine, the rain in my fall and the joy in my tears. I love you!

To my sisters: Meena, Yolanda and Adrienne. I want you to know that I love you all the same. You remind me of mommy in every way. I want you to know that I am praying for you always. I am proud to be your little brother and if I'm spoiled it's your fault! I am the youngest and only boy! I do what I do because of you.

My prayer is that I become successful. That I can bless your lives that you'd never lack anything. Thank you for the memories and all of my nieces and nephews. They cause me to smile and live each day. Thank you (Nug), Thank you (Gabby), Thank you, (Beg). I love you!

To my nieces and nephews, I am proud of you. You all have a special place in my heart, which no one else can fill. I remember when you were born, when I found out, and the joy I felt. Every time I held you, changed you, encouraged you, heard your concerns, saw your tears and most of all watched your personalities develop, have all been priceless moments.

Kaheim, Kiana, De 'Andre, D'Ana, D' Marco, Keyon and D' Mira, know that you are loved. I am expecting the best from all of you. Know that "Uncle Man" as you all call me, will always be here for you. I'm never too busy or too far away that you cannot reach me.

Pave your own futures. Live life to the fullest and whenever someone says: "You can't!" smile at them and say: "I can do all things through Christ that strengthens me." Philippians 413.

To my aunt, Carolyn Wright, "auntie." There aren't enough pages in this book to convey how I feel about you. If it wasn't for your investing in my future and planting seeds of encouragement into my life, only God knows where I would be.

You have always been my number one supporter. When I had no one to talk to, you became my therapist and your home became my therapy room. If walks could talk, they'd speak of our conversations, our just us moments, my secrets, our laughs, and shared tears. You are God's greatest secret. The world needs to know who you are. You have so much to offer and it is my prayer that you live as long as you want and never want as long as you live. I love you!

To my aunts Bell and Barbara, I love you! I want you to know that over the years you have come through some tough times and the Lord was there to see you through it all. I'm proud of the women you've become, keep loving, keep laughing and most of all keep living!

To "Uncle Junior," (Anderson Wright Sr.) Thank you for the love and concern you showed me when my father passed away. I know you miss your little brother as I do. I pray for you constantly, you too are loved.

To all of my cousins: Erica, Charlene, Stevie, Nicole, Lamont, Toi, Amber, La'Quan, Azalia, Deidra, Tanisha, Juan, Joseph, Tony, Lisa, Vickie, Christina, Christopher, Milton, Charles, Anderson, Carissa, Anton, Diane, Jimmy, Karima, Christine, Lawanda, Olivia and Mattie Ruth, I love ya'll to life.

To the world's greatest friends: Chasson Wingate, Alonso Alston, Latasha McIver, Fern Gilford, Kim Jackson, Michael Pittman Jr., Carolyn Lett-Youman, Tiffany Pinckney, Ryan Petgrave, Fred Martin III, Martin McFadden, Sharmaine Byrd, Ernest Spellman, Keisha Spellman, Gregory Williams, Tiva Williams, Vanessa Riley, Brian D. Coats, Kenneth McDuffie, Sandra X Santiago, Jennifer Hayes, Karinthia Taylor and Terry 'Coopie' Cooper. I love ya'll. You are priceless and non-refundable.

To those who have inspired me in ministry, including but not limited to: Dr. Gerald G. Seabrooks, Dr. Sonia Curmon, Reverend John L. Pratt Sr., Pastor Carolyn King, Prophet Andre Cook, Bishop Iona E. Locke, Bishop Clinton L. Heyward, Prophet Charles E. Brown, Pastor Adrienne Exum-Johnson, Overseer Anitera Newell, Ambassador Glenda Phillips-Lee, Overseer Maurice Flythe, Pastor Latonya Heyward, Elder Susan Webley Cox, Evangelist Julia Gilford, Pastor Jonathan and

Janice Welfare, Pastor Ifeachor Potts, and the churches and ministries you all represent, I thank you.

To my bishop, Bishop George L. Bennett, Overseer Martha Bennett, Kingdom Connection Ministries and Hupernikao Fellowship of Churches, I love and appreciate you. I thank God for you always. He has privileged me to work alongside some of the greatest Kingdom builders. We are more than conquerors, we have surpassing victory, we are one, and we are blessed! #Hupernikao4life!

I would like to also give a special thank you to my sister and friend Pastor Alicia M. Collins and the Gates of Praise Ministries. For years you have been an inspiration to me. You have pushed me literally beyond limits. You always encouraged me to see past my present me to my future me. We've laughed together, cried together, fought together and we're still standing! – In the words of singer-songwriter Andrew Gold: "Thank you for being a friend."

To my godmother, Gloria G. Stewart. I am grateful to God for you. I mean what could I possibly say, other than thank you and I love you. You have always been an encouragement to me. We've traveled many roads together. You served me and checked me at the same time. I am proud of you, be encouraged and know that, eyes have not seen, nor ear heard, neither have entered into the heart of man, the things which God hath prepared for them (You, Gloria Stewart) that love Him (God)!

To Francesca Norsen Tate, you are truly a Godsend. You are a tremendous blessing to me. You are a reminder of

Phoebe of whom Apostle Paul talks in scripture. Someone who was blessed and was able to bless him as he embarked on ministry. Thank you. I am eternally grateful!

To all of the L.I.F.E. Class participants, to those of you who call me pastor, to Kingdom Building Victorious Church, thank you for trusting the God in me to help you start again, to help us live again, love you! Thank you Leslie Smith for those constant Kingdom reminders.

And finally, to my gift. On Friday, April 25, 2014 – A champion was born, my champion was born – Karter Myles. Welcome into the world, Champ. Because of you the world has become a better place. "Lo, children are a gift from the Lord: and the fruit of the womb is his reward." Psalm 127:3.

# TABLE OF CONTENTS

# FOREWORD

During the past 30 years, my work as a religion editor for a community newspaper has brought me in touch with many different churches, pastors, ministers, as well as faithful and doubting Christians alike. But not even this professional experience could have prepared me for my own spiritual crisis – the deep, dark grief surrounding my husband's death.

When I met Pastor LeeAndrew Wright, he taught me that, in struggling through life's most painful moments, I am not alone. People all around me are carrying similar burdens of grief, pain, and anxiety. But most importantly, Pastor Wright taught me that God is steadfast in providing help. Call it Life Support. Drawing on his many creative talents, Pastor Wright taught me that God is ever-present, and that I *can* find God's grace and hope in the struggle.

As I read each of the devotionals in *Critical Grace*, my faith has increased and I have found renewed purpose in my own work to teach readers about the importance of loving those most different from ourselves.

Each of the stories in *Critical Grace: Living on God's Life's Support* speaks to experiences of pain and joy. As you read, many of the situations that unfold in this book may resonate with you. I hope you find peace, insight and even joy in the redemption that God sends into each of these stories.

As you read and meditate on *Critical Grace*, you may also find yourself wanting to revisit these stories many times. God's timing is anything but linear. Often, He gives us a new piece of the puzzle of life when He, in His wisdom, believes we are ready. These stories are like the puzzle pieces. Each time you will understand the story in a new way. May *Critical Grace* give you abundant blessings in your own life.

Francesca N. Tate
Religion Editor
The Brooklyn Eagle

# TIMES UP

There is a famous saying that many have quoted through-out the centuries. Many of you reading this devotional may be guilty of saying it yourself without knowing the revelation or understanding behind it: *"When life gives you lemons, make lemonade."*

When looking at the beauty of a lemon the first thing most people would notice is the brightness of the fruit. The artistry of its shape and its color normally attracts people to it. This fruit, with its multiple purposes is a popular one among apples, oranges and grapes, but unlike other fruits that are sweet to the taste, the lem-on, once bitten into leaves a bitter taste on the palates of the tongue.

Do you remember the first time you bit into a lemon? Do you remember the taste of its bitterness, that sour taste that made you say, *"I'm not going to eat that again?"*

Yeah, I know you do. Many of you right now, just the thought of the memory causes your mouth to salivate and your tongue feels as if you can taste it right now.

Well that's how life is. Though God blesses us and causes us to live a fruitful life, sometimes we get more lemons than apples, more limes than oranges and more kiwis than strawberries.

Sometimes life can put you into a place where you'll ask God, *"What am I to do with this?"* Life can cause you to become bitter if you don't learn to take what has been given to you and make something out of it.

Many of us made the statement, we'd never eat a lemon again. Most have had a change of heart since we learned what purpose the lemon serves, and how we can truly benefit from it if we use it wisely.

The one thing I like about lemons is once the lemon is peeled and its seeds removed, you can take the lemon and squeeze it, this now produces lemon juice. Afterwards you take the lemon juice, put it into a pitcher, add to it some water and a little sugar, stir it all together, add a few ice cubes, and you'll have a refreshing drink called lemonade, that can be shared with others.

That's what life is all about. Taking the one thing that would normally work against you, finding purpose for it and making it work for you. Once you learn its purpose, it is your responsibility to take what you've learned and share your experience with others.

I remember as a child growing up, I would go on school trips. These school trips would sometimes be to a local farm where we would pick fruit. We would be handed baskets by our teacher and told, *"Here's your basket, you are responsible for it, and I am expecting you to return these baskets back to me by the end of the day. Remember, children: you can have as much fruit as your basket can carry."*

By the end of the day I would have filled my basket with as much fruit as my little arms could hold. I knew there was someone at home who could take the fruit that I labored all day to pick and make something out of it.

I knew my grandmother could take the apples and make apple pies, my dad could take the oranges and make orange juice and that my mom could take the peaches and make preserves. All while picking those fruits, I thought of how good it would be to wake up in the morning, knowing that the oranges that were used to make the juice for breakfast, I had picked.

Life is a trip, it's but for a moment. God has given each and every one of us our own basket and He's saying, like my teacher once said: *"Here's your basket, you are responsible for it, and I am expecting you to return these baskets back to me by the end of the day. Remember, children: you can have as much fruit as your basket can carry."*

That's what God has done with us. He has handpicked us and placed us in His basket. He has made us all into different individuals, for all different purposes. Now it is our duty to use the purpose of which we've been picked to serve one another.

Remember, when God gives you an assignment, it's never about you. It's about Him and what it is He wants to accomplish upon the earth. He uses us to get the job done! I always tell people in Christ, *"You just may be the basket He's using for the picking."*

I know it sounds a little country; however, what it means is that we, the church, are the baskets that God entrusts to carry the fruit – the souls, the lives that He has handpicked. It is our job to take that which has been given to us, cultivate it, develop it, teach it, and prepare it for what it is God wants it to be.

In Matthew 25:13-30, Jesus gives us a parable of the talents or money, if you will. He starts off with an introduction: *"Therefore stay alert, because you do not know the day or the hour, for it is like a man going on a journey, who summoned his slaves and entrusted his property to them."*

He goes on to say, *"To one he gave five talents, to another two, and to another one, each according to his ability."* Whenever God is distributing talents to individuals, know that He gives it according to the individual's ability. What He gives one, He may not give another.

When the Lord gave these men their talents, He gave them these talents expecting them to bring increase and not excuses! The one who had received five talents went off right away and put his money to work and guaranteed five more. In the same way, the one who had two gained two more, but the one who had received one talent went out and dug a hole in the ground and hid his master's money in it.

What have you done with the talents in *your* life? Have you taken what was given to you and brought increase or have you taken your talents and *buried* them?

Some people ask me this question all the time: *"How do I know my life's purpose?"* or *"How do I know what my talent(s) are?"* My response to them is this: *"You'll know what your purpose in life is, when you start to do what you love and what you love (your natural talent) starts to bring you increase and success.* Natural talent once perfected, cultivated and invested in, can bring you success and great gain.

We have to learn how to operate quickly in that which the Lord has given us. We never know when He's going to come and require at our hand an account of that which He has entrusted *into* our hands.

After a long time, the master of those slaves came and settled his accounts with them. The one who had received the five talents came and brought five more, saying, *'Sir, you entrusted me with five talents. See, I have gained five more.'* His master answered, *'Well done, good and faithful slave! You have been faithful in a few things. I will put you in charge of many things. Enter into the joy of your master.'*

The one with the two talents also came and said, *'Sir, you entrusted two talents to me. See, I have gained two more.'* His master answered, *'Well done, good and faithful slave! You have been faithful in a few things. I will put you in charge of many things. Enter into the joy of your master.'*

So you see, whenever you are obedient and take the talent(s) that God has given you and cause those talents to yield an increase for Him, not only are you commended, you are also promoted! However, sometimes things don't always work out the way we plan them.

Fear, a distressing emotion aroused by impending danger, evil or pain – whether real or imagined – can cause you to forfeit all that God has for you, like the slave, who had received the one talent.

*"Sir, I knew that you were a hard man, harvesting where you did not sow and gathering where you did not scatter seed, so I was afraid, and I went and hid your talent in the ground. See, you have what is yours.'* But his master answered, *'Evil and lazy slave! So you knew that I harvest where I didn't sow and gathered where I didn't scatter? Then you should have deposited my money with the bankers, and on my return I would have received my money back with interest! Therefore, take the talent from him and give it to the one who has ten!"*

In Ecclesiastes 3, Solomon deals with something called time. He starts off by saying, *"There is an appointed time for everything. And there is a time for every event under heaven."* The key word in this statement is *'time,'* and it is used thirty times within the first eight verses of chapter 3.

Solomon also builds his argument upon the word *'appointed.'* Letting us know that the events of our lives do not randomly happen, but God has a *'purpose'* behind them. Solomon also uses an unusual Hebrew word translated *"event."* This word conveys the idea of *"delight."* In other words, there is a sense of success based on appropriate timing. Again, *timing* is everything!

Therefore, because the slave with the one talent took it and buried it, God turned around and said, *"For the one who has will be given more and he will have more than enough. But the one who does not have, even what he has will be taken from him. And throw that worthless slave into the outer darkness, where there will be weeping and gnashing of teeth!"*

Why? Because the man didn't take his *'time'* seriously. He allowed fear to mulct his *'purpose'* and instead of taking *'delight'* in that which the Lord had given him and make use of his *'appointed'* time, he buried it and made excuses. Because of that not only did he lose his talent but he also lost his place with God.

Faithful service leads to increased responsibilities in the kingdom of heaven, and eternal joy in the presence of our Master, Jesus Christ. However, unfaithful service leads to condemnation, the removal of one's stewardship, and an eternity of weeping and gnashing of teeth in outer darkness, away from the presence of the Lord.

This slave allowed his fear to cause him to relinquish his talents because he was afraid to take the lemons given to him and make lemonade. Remember, your talents and abilities were given to you by God to use for your own benefit, for the benefit of others and to bring praise and glory to Him. So whatever you do, do your very best, for yourself, for others and for God.

Do it *delightfully, purposely and timely.* You never want to hear God say, *"Time's up!"* and you haven't accomplished what it is He called you do. Time is of the essence.

## The Word:

- Exodus 31:1-11
- Ecclesiastes 3:1-8
- Matthew 25:13-30
- Luke 25:13-30
- 1 Peter 4:10-11
- Ephesians 5:15-17
- Psalm 90:12
- Colossians 4:5
- James 4:13-17
- Psalm 39:4-5
- John 9:4
- Psalm 31:14-15
- 2 Peter 3:8-14
- Matthew 24:36
- Ecclesiastes 12:1-5
- Habakkuk 2:3
- Isaiah 60:22
- Acts 17:31
- Proverbs 10:7
- 2 Peter 3:3-9
- 2 Corinthians 3:5-6
- Proverbs 20:13
- Proverbs 10:4
- 1 Corinthians 3:13

## The Prayer:

"Father, it's in the Name of Jesus that I come to you today. Lord I pray that you would forgive me for not making proper use of the time that you have given me. I repent for being laggard and lazy concerning the things of God.

Please, forgive me and try me all over again. It is my delight to serve you and to do your will! Lord, I will purpose in my heart to do that which you have appointed me to do and I will do it faithfully and in a timely manner, knowing that in You, I'll have my reward. This I pray in Jesus' Name, Amen."

# CHANGE LOOKS
# GOOD ON ME

I asked the Lord, *"How am I going to recover from this?"* His response to me was, *"Change!"* Whenever one thinks of having to change something in their life, it's always faced with resistance.

Being that we are all creatures of habit, once we indulge in a thing for any period of time, it tends to become second nature to us. Therefore, causing this trichotomy of man to always war within us.

When I think of change, I think of coins, yes coins! Whenever you take a dollar and make a purchase, normally the purchaser receives change back from the clerk. Most people don't like to carry around a lot of change, especially when given pennies. Ask most people what they do with the change they are given, and the will say, *"I give it to the grandchildren,"* or they'll say, *"I keep it in a jar at home,"* or in the cup holder of their car.

Why? Because change is heavy. My God, change, when carried loosely and in great quantity, makes a lot of noise. Change normally makes sounds that draw unnecessary attention. People can hear you as you walk by, depending on how much change you have in your pocket. But what most people don't realize is that even though change is loud and heavy, it carries as much value as a dollar bill once added together.

One day at church it was announced that we would be having a building fund. Every member was asked to donate a certain amount of money by the end of the year to help toward our building fund. Everyone was excited about the new project and was looking forward to the end of the year so that we could see what the church wanted to purchase.

That Sunday, after church, I went to my godfather's house and in his basement I found and old water cooler bottle. I asked him if it was okay for me to have the water bottle, and his reply was, *"What in the world could you want with an old water bottle?"* My response to him was; *"I need it for a project."* He said, with a look of flurry on his face, *"be my guest."*

When I went home that day, I took out a marker and wrote on the water bottle, *'Nehemiah Building Fund Project.'* Right under that I wrote down my goal. I was a college student at the time and I could barely afford my tuition, much less give to a building fund. But I was determined to sacrifice and give, so that the house of the Lord could have what it needed.

Whenever I'd spend a dollar, I'd take the change that was given back to me and place it into the water bottle. Six months had gone by and I noticed that the water bottle wasn't even halfway full. That's when doubt kicked in and I said, *"I never should have made that pledge!"* I knew Ecclesiastes 5:5 says, *"Far better not to vow in the first place than to vow and not pay up."*

11

My emotions got the best of me, and I started to worry that I would be a fool of words rather than a man of action. That is when the war began. The enemy in my inner self began to say those four little words we all dread to hear, *"I told you so!"*

My spirit became grieved and I thought to myself, *"I can't do it!"* My soul was in turmoil; my emotions were everywhere. I just couldn't seem to figure out how I was going to keep my vow. My mind kept saying, *"They'll understand. You're a college student. You're broke!"* But my spirit kept telling me, *"I can do all things through Christ who strengthens me!"*

While the war was waging on the inside of my spirit, the water cooler that looked so promising, now just looked half empty, with no chance of fulfillment. What was supposed to be so easy to accomplish, now cause me to feel oppressed. I became *depressed* because of the *suppression* I felt. Knowing that man is made up of three parts: Body, Soul and Spirit, and that they're always battling, my body soon became the referee between my soul and my spirit.

The spirit is the seat of man's thoughts, the mental aspect. I Corinthians 2:11, *"For who knows a person's thoughts except the spirit of that person, which is in him? So also no one comprehends the thoughts of God except the Spirit of God."*

The soul is the emotions, the heart of the person. John 6:63, *"It is the spirit that gives life; the flesh profits nothing: the words that I speak unto you, they are spirit, and they are life."* Once I realized that I was torn between my body, soul and spirit, I felt like David in Psalm 42:5, *"Why are you in despair, O my soul? And why have you become disturbed within me? Hope in God, for I shall again praise Him for the help of his presence."*

With that I looked at the water cooler again and the Lord said to me, *"In order for you to not allow yourself to be defeated, you have to change!"*

When I went to church that following Sunday, I was asked how my pledge was coming along. I looked at the trustee of the church and said, *"It's coming,"* then I walked away. A few people who were standing there when the question was asked, looked at each other and said, *"Ump, poor thing, he's about to drown himself. Always jumping into things head first!"*

After church I went to my godfather's house. While preparing dinner, he asked a similar question that the trustee asked just moments before, *"How's your project coming along?"*

I looked at him and said, *"Not so well."* He then asked me what the problem was. I told him about the building fund and my goal; that it didn't look like it was going to happen. He looked at me, handed me some potatoes and said, *"Here son, peel and pray."* I looked at him like he was crazy, but did what I was told.

While peeling and praying I thought about what the trustee asked and what the people said. The story of David came to mind. In 1 Samuel 30, David and his men approached the city of Ziklag. They are horrified to see that the city has been destroyed and their families taken captive. No one was killed, but every living soul was taken. It is of little comfort that their families are still alive.

Each man imagines what happened or will happen to his wife and children. At best, they will become slaves, to be worked hard and cruelly treated. At worst...no one even wanted to consider this.

David's two wives are also taken and the 600 men are greatly distressed by what has happened to their city and their families. They weep until they have no sobs left. They begin to think about how this came to be. It had been David's plan to bring them to the land of the Philistines. It was David's request that they live in this remote city of Ziklag, and it was David who led them off to fight with the Philistines, leaving their families vulnerable to attack. Some were so angry they talked about stoning David.

David says to Abiathar the priest, Ahimelech's son, *"This I pray you, bring me the ephod."* And Abiathar brings him the ephod. David inquires of the Lord saying, *"Shall I pursue this troop? Shall I overtake them?"* The Lord answers him, *"Pursue, for you shall surely over take them and without fail recover all."*

Before I knew it, the peeled potatoes had become potato salad and dinner was almost done. My godfather posed another question, *"What did the Lord say about your project?"* I replied, *"He showed me the story of David and his men at Ziklag, and He told me to change!"* That's it He wants me to *change!* Change the way I'm looking at the situation, and handling what I was going through!

That night I left my godfather's house with a jar of coins he'd been keeping on his dresser. He told me he hated change because change was noisy and heavy. But, the *change* he *didn't want*, was the *change* that *I needed!*

In life there is going to come a time when change is required. No matter how heavy it is to carry or how much noise it makes when you walk by. The weight of the change is necessary to help you build up strength and muscle. Moreover, that change must be noisy so that when others hear you coming, not only will they *hear* you, they'll be able to *see* your change and its *value.*

But, the change doesn't come until *you* change. It wasn't until David changed his clothes, that he got an answer. By changing out of his war clothes and into his priestly garments David was able to seek the Lord. The Lord saw his change, heard his prayer and gave him instructions. David changed his way of thinking on how to pursue that which he needed to conquer.

David was a man of trichotomy, he was made up of body, soul and spirit. However, David was also a godly man, who was a prophet, priest and king. Had David listened to the men and just went after their enemy who'd taken their wives, children and possessions, it is a strong possibility David and his men would have lost the pursuit – because they would've been in the flesh.

15

But because David took off his war clothes and put on his priestly garments, he was able to seek the Lord concerning pursuing his enemies. The response David received from the Lord was more than he could ever ask for. The Lord told David, not only would David *pursue*, but that David in his men would surely *overtake them* and *without fail recover all!*

I'm here to encourage you, to tell you, now that *you've* taken off your war clothes, removed *your* doubting garments, and sought *the Lord*, not only will you *pursue*, but you *shall* surely *overtake* your goals and *without fail* recover all that you've lost!

This next ministry assignment in your life will be without fail. I know that you feel as if you've failed in your past, but that was then and this is now! You've made it to Ziklag and the providence of God has given you more than your mouth could ever ask or your heart desire. Ephesians 3:20, *"Now unto Him who is able to do immeasurably, more than all we ask or imagine, according to his power that is at work within us."*

The providence of God is His *unseen* hand in the events of your life. Assuring and achieving His purpose and promises. David had been chosen and anointed as Israel's next king. God protected him and provided for him and his men in amazing ways – ways we could not necessarily recognize as such at the time they are happening.

David in his men not only obtained their own goods back, but also the goods of many others. David shared his spoil with a number of Israelite towns, thus ingratiating him to these kinsmen. Ziklag was burned to the ground, the only unrecoverable loss. Yet this *"loss"* was instrumental in David to return to the land of Judah, where he was made *King of Judah.*

All things do truly work together for the good, to those who love God, to those who are the called according to His purpose. Had I listened to the crowd who said I was always *'jumping into things head first,'* or looked at my situation and gave up on my vow, I wouldn't know what it was to have made it to my own Ziklag and to know that the *challenge* was really in the *change!* Thank you Lord, for my *change!*

| The Word: |
|:---:|

- Romans 8:28
- Ecclesiastes 5:5
- Philippians 4:11-13
- 1 Corinthians 2:11
- Psalm 46:1
- Psalm 42:5
- John 6:63
- James 5:6
- 1 Samuel 30
- Ephesians 3:20
- Proverbs 3:5-6
- Psalm 37:4-6
- Psalm 9:10

- Psalm 28:7
- Romans 12:19
- Psalm 91:1-16
- John 10:10
- Jeremiah 17:7-8
- Psalm 144:1
- Psalm 40:1-17
- Job 13:15
- Proverbs 24:10
- Psalm 119:165

## The Prayer:

"Father, I thank You for Your loving kindness and Your tender mercies. I thank You for being a patient God! Thank You for not allowing me to make rash decisions, but for giving me the wisdom to come to You, and seek You for guidance.

I know that without You I am nothing, but with You I can do all things! Now God, let patience work her perfect work in me, so that after I come through these trials, I will be mature and complete, not in want of anything. In Jesus' Name, I pray. Amen."

# A CONVERSATION
# WITH GRACE AND MERCY

Have you ever felt like you were in this world alone? Felt as if you were banished into the wilderness, far away from reality and that you were somehow meant to learn something while going through this season of loneliness, but you didn't quite get it?

While in this wilderness, in the darkness of a cave, you felt as if you were consumed by the terror of night. Fear gripped you, and you felt as if all hope was lost?

Depression crept in, while sadness moved in. Joy walked out and along with it peace; and in its suitcase went love, temperance, longsuffering, meekness, gentleness, faith and goodness. Just when tears began to flow down your face, there was a knock of sunshine coming toward the darkness of your cave, and what you heard uplifted you. You heard a still small voice asking, *"Is there anybody in here?"*

Could it be? Finally, the Lord has come! He has sent help from the sanctuary, strength out of Zion! Had someone seen me when I became shipwrecked and in despair? Had someone seen my distress call, my SOS? – *(Sobs-Out-of-my-Soul)*.

There goes that voice again, this time it sounds a little stronger. It sounds a bit hopeful. Here comes that light again. *"Yes, yes, there is someone in here!"* I say, but this time there is no response.

Did I imagine this whole thing? Have I been in this cave of despair for so long that I've started to hallucinate? Thinking that there is hope, when there is no help beyond the darkness of what I can see? Is it time for me to die? I ask myself aloud. Only to hear my own voice, a voice of doom, and echo back toward the ears of the mouth that had spoken it.

*Oh no! What did I say?* I must remember that death and life are in the power of the tongue. I began to pray, to hope against hope – to call on the Lord for help. To help me see beyond the darkness that surrounded me, to help me see that *there was* light beyond this grave, that *there was* peace beyond this storm, that *there was* joy beyond this pain. I need faith to overcome my fears.

Help me to believe, I asked the Lord. Help me to believe that *there is* rest after my suffering. That I'd be a bit meeker *after this* parry, and that His love for me would come and rescue me from the pits of anguish that I was feeling. That temperance would find its way through the excess of alienation I was feeling.

My soul overwhelmed and my heart broken asunder, my mind in a state of perplexity, uncertainty, I asked the question, *"What am I to do?"* This stronghold has overtaken me. I'm in a cave called Adullam.

As I drifted off to sleep, I heard those voices again. This time the voices are louder and more determined. The cave becomes filled with noise. Had I dreamt the whole thing? Am I *not* in a cave after all? Am I *not* alone?

*"Yes, you're in a cave, but no, you are not alone,"* the voices say. *"We've been here with you all this time. Allow us to introduce ourselves. He's Grace and he's Mercy,"* they say pointing one to the other.

*"We showed up when you first called out for help, but we couldn't find you. Your faith became weak and it couldn't lead us to you."* Grace said.

*"But when you began to pray again, your faith spoke to us and said, 'follow me, he's this way!' "* Mercy added.

*"You're running from the very reason for which you exist, for which you were born. The enemy is trying to take your purpose and kill your destiny!"* Grace said.

*"We were sent to find you. You see, you were born for this! God had spoken it from the beginning of time. Before the Lord formed you in your mother's womb. He knew you! He sanctified you!"* Mercy added.

*"He ordained you a prophet to the nations!"* they said.

*"But I am nothing but a concubine's kid. How could I be sanctified and called a prophet to the nation, when my own father's ashamed of me? Look, Mercy, I was shaped in iniquity, and not only that, Grace, it was in sin that my mother conceived me,"* I said.

21

*"But that doesn't disqualify you from what it is God has ordained you to be. You see, He knew all of that when He called you. So is it His word that goes out of His mouth; it will not return unto Him void, but will accomplish what He desires and achieve, the purpose of which He sent it!"* Mercy replied.

*"Now you see why you can't stay in this cave? This cave wasn't mean to hold you, it was meant to house you, until you got yourself together! Not only is the Lord expecting you to make it, but look – look at all those people out there waiting on you – God's chosen!"* Grace continued, pointing to the entrance of the cave.

*"Listen, He wants you to know that the thoughts that He think toward you, are thoughts of peace, and not of evil, to give you an expected end. Now get up from here, you have people waiting on you – cheering you on!"* Mercy said.

*"They are? All those people are waiting for me?"* I asked.

*"Why yes, the creation waits in eager expectation for the sons of God to be revealed! Now, come on!* They said dragging him out of the cave.

*"You have a destiny waiting on you, a kingdom – a people, a purpose! And remember, we will follow you all the days of your life – even when it seems we're not here, we are!"* they said, as their voices faded into eternity.

*"Okay, I'm ready to go,"* I said.

As I walked toward the mouth of the cave, I became fully aware that I wasn't alone after all. There in front of me stood some of the greatest destiny pushers that I could have ever hoped for. They waited patiently, while I came to myself. While my faith and hope came back. While I took a retrospective look within. I looked back to thank Grace and Mercy; and just like that, they were gone, but somehow I knew they were there.

*How could I have been surrounded by all of these people but yet felt all alone?* I asked myself.

When I approached the entrance of the cave, someone reached over and handed me a stack of neatly arranged papers. I asked, *"What are these?"*

The young, cheery voice replied, *"These are yours. While you were in this cave, you began to write down what it is you were feeling. Every time you finished, I would take the papers and neatly arrange them. I took some twine and tied them together for you – I thought you'd want to have them, so I saved them."*

*"Thank you. Now let's go, destiny awaits,"* I said to the lad.

Sometimes life will put you on a run. A run from yourself, a run from what surrounds you and, sometimes a run from your enemies. You're not running away from your enemies because you're afraid of what they might do to you – no – you're running away because of what you might do to them, especially when your enemy is someone you love.

Jesus reminds us in Matthew 5:44, *"But I tell you: Love your enemies, bless them that curse you, do good to them that hate you, and pray for those who despitefully use you, and persecute you."*

In order to keep our hands clean, we like David and his band of 600 men have to hide in caves. Not just any cave, but a cave in limestone clefts, with lush vegetation, fresh water springs and waterfalls. These caves were a natural refuge and provided a lookout spot from which to see an enemy approaching. Isn't it amazing that while you are on the run from the enemy, God would still provide the best for you?

Saul was committed to killing David and was still pursuing him assiduously. But there comes a time when God will put your enemy right in front of you to see what *you* would do. If given the chance, would you render evil for evil or bless them in spite of? David was able to restrain himself from killing Saul, but he couldn't resist the temptation to cut off some of Saul's robe.

We often do the same to those who have hurt us, with a little cut here and a little jab there. Cutting off Saul's robe may have felt good at the moment, but it didn't mend David's hurt. Healing, however came for David when he confronted Saul with the truth.

"Why do you listen when people say, 'David wants to ruin you?' he asked Saul. 'Look! Today your own eyes have seen that the Lord handed you over to me in the cave. But I refused to kill you. I spared you. I won't lift a hand against my master, because he is the Lord's anointed."

"Look here, my protector!" He goes on to say. "See the corner of your robe is in my hand. I cut off the corner of your robe but didn't kill you. So know now that I am not guilty of wrongdoing or rebellion. I haven't wronged you, but you are hunting me down, trying to kill me."

Then David really entreats him with empathy by telling him, "May the Lord judge between me and you! May the Lord take vengeance on you for me!" David knew that he had been anointed for a special purpose. It seemed obvious to everyone that he would be the next king. There was a golden opportunity to kill Saul and take the throne as the rightful leader. But because God is Omnipotent (*All Powerful*), Omnipresent (*All Seeing*), and Omniscient (*All Knowing*), He never left David *Hopeless, Helpless, or Useless!* He already knew David's future.

Maybe you found yourself in a cave, hiding, afraid. Afraid to the point that you were willing to run away and forfeit who you are because of someone else's jealousy, someone else's rage or envy. But thank God you didn't! Precious heart, it is time for you to come out of your cave!

I know – I know. I've been there before myself; we've all been lied on and mistreated at some point, especially those of us who are *really* anointed. You see, it comes with the territory! Being anointed doesn't mean you don't have to fight. When you are anointed, you have to learn to fight skillfully – know your enemy.

Never let your enemy see you cry. As a matter of fact, when given the chance, confront him or her. Let them know how their actions affected you. Let them know that what was meant for your evil, God has turned it around for your good.

What was supposed to kill you, only caused you to live. Your purpose may have changed, but your destiny will always remain the same. You have no more time to waste – get up from where you are and live! – Destiny awaits!

| The Word: |
| --- |

- Proverbs 18:21
- Matthew 5:44
- Romans 8:19
- Romans 12:19
- Jeremiah 29:11
- Jeremiah 1:10
- Psalm 20:2
- Psalm 34:4
- Psalm 41:11
- Psalm 75:7
- Galatians 5:22-23
- 1 Samuel 16:23
- 1 Samuel 24
- Esther 2:16-17
- Jeremiah 31:2-3
- Hebrews 4:16
- Romans 8:31

- Isaiah 53:4-6
- Luke 6:22
- Psalm 34:18
- Psalm 55:22
- Philippians 4:13

| The Prayer: |
| --- |

Father I thank You that You didn't leave me to my own thoughts. You saw in me what I couldn't see in myself. Thank You for the favor that is on my life. Thank You that You didn't leave me hopeless, helpless or useless, but in Your own infinite wisdom looked beyond my faults and saw my need.

Thank You, Father, for not allowing me to stay in a place of depression and misery. But You sent grace and mercy to find me while I was hiding in darkness and allowed them to carry me into Your marvelous light.

Thank You, kind Sir, for being Omnipotent, Omniscient and Omnipresent. Strong and Mighty, everywhere at the same time, and never absent from anywhere! In Jesus' Name, I pray, Amen."

# THERE IS AN AFTER THIS

What happens when your promises are tied to tears? What happens when the armor that has been handed to you to protect yourself, leave you vulnerable for attack, because it's too big for you to wear?

What happens when you find yourself in a drought and the only meal that you're receiving is being fed to you by dirty hands? What happens when *God* brings you out of something that was meant to destroy you; yet you turn around and become salty and bitter?

You didn't understand, God loved you so much so that He destroyed it, so that *you* could no longer have access to it.

How do we begin to live again when we come home and find that which you love is now gone; and the enemy has plundered through your home and stolen your most prized possessions, kidnapped your children and captured your spouse? How do you hold on to faith when whores have houses and thieves have dens, yet you yourself are homeless and down to your last? – So, you decided to bake some bread, close your eyes and await death, just to wake up in the morning from hunger pains reminding you, you're still alive?

What happens when your name has been changed so

that others can forget who you are? What happens when the person who was supposed to help you, turns around and steals your inheritance? What happens when you go from Debar, a place where, as you speak things happen – to Lo-Debar – a place of no word?

What happens when the person who was meant to carry you, drops you in their haste, and their hasty decision caused you to be handicapped? It's okay – the King is coming. He is coming not based on a prophecy, but a promise. He's coming to show not his enemy but his friend some kindness.

Mira-Baal [an opponent of Baal] whose father was a prince and grandfather a king, now finds himself lowlier than sand because of a name change, to Mephibosheth, which means destroying shame. Have you ever suffered from an identity crisis? A crisis where you were torn between who you really are and what you had become?

Some event may have caused you to be traumatized and removed you from your *was* to what *is,* and what *is* seems to outweigh what *was.* Now you're living your life in the shadows of shame and rejection, humiliation and pain. You feel embarrassed, ostracized and criticized because everyone's learned of your secret shame – the shame that you thought you hid so well.

That's how Mephibosheth felt. His grandfather, Saul, disobeyed God. King Saul tried to kill David whom God had chosen to be king, numerous times. King Saul went to a witch to see if he could get some spiritual advice. As a result, Saul died, and so did Mira-Baal's dad, Prince Jonathan. Mira-Baal, now *Mephibosheth*, for years was left to fend for himself.

Mephibosheth was five years old when his father Jonathan, David's best friend, was killed in battle. So Mephibosheth, a baby prince, whose life should have been filled with wealth, became a life of tragedy, heartbreak and misery. He became a crippled beggar, living as an orphan in hiding. While his family was being assassinated, murdered and banished, his future as a promising king would never be fulfilled.

Mephibosheth went from being a prince to a pauper, from royalty to rags, from the kingdom to the gutter, from the penthouse to the basement. Mephibosheth, the son of Jonathan and grandson of Saul, was dropped as a child by the nurse whose job it was to take care of him.

The nurse received news that King Saul had lost and died in battle, along with the men of war; and among those men was Jonathan, the king's son. But even in the death of her king, she realized that the future and promise of the kingdom were left in her hands. Without second thought, and in her haste to flee approaching death, she picked up Mira-Baal and she ran.

She ran until she could no longer see the enemy trailing behind them. She ran until she felt danger was no more. But when she ran, she didn't run alone. Her loyalty was to her king and so when she ran, she ran with the *heir to the throne in her arms. She picked up the fragile package that read, "Handle with care!"* She took Mira-Baal and while running she dropped the package. Just like that, the package *Mira-Baal* is broken!

She didn't mean to drop him. She was trying to be loyal. Her goal was to take the child and flee to safety. Where could they go? Surely they would be looking for the lad. Everybody knew that Mira-Baal was a favored child. She knew that they would be looking for him to kill him, as he is the heir to the throne. In order to protect him she knew that she had to take him to a place where no one knew who he was or question where he came from. There must be a place where the king's enemies won't be able to find us. *Lo-Debar, that's it we can go to Lo-Debar!*

Lo-Debar, does that place sound familiar? The name alone draws an eerie conclusion. It speaks with such finality. Though Mira-Baal is dropped by trusted hands, I can say I really can't blame the nurse, after all she was a nurse, not his guardian. She should never have been placed in that predicament. Fate required her to become a bodyguard.

Like Mephibosheth who trusted his nurse, some of us can relate to being dropped by those in whom we've placed our trust. We're living crippling lives because a person whom we loved and gave our trust to has dropped us. Our lives are still suffering from the crippling effects of those disappointments.

However, everyone has been *dropped* in some way.

31

Sometimes those whom we trust to take care of and protect us end up hurting us instead. Many times they are keeping us from blessings and not harm – as was the case with Mephibosheth.

They were running from the blessings and not from harm. This has great implications for the lost as well as the saved in the world. People who are lost in the world are running from the blessings of God, and then questioning and even blaming Him when things go wrong. If you were Mephibosheth, would you be asking God, why He let you fall and get crippled? Would you blame God?

Many times in my own life, looking back, I can see where the bad points in my life happened when I was running from God and His blessings. Now in Mephibosheth's defense we see that the family's trustee has taken the inheritance for himself and his family, because of Mira-Baal, Mephibosheth's situation. However, when the King comes, not only will he the trustee have to give back what he stole, God is going to make Mira-Baal's defrauders serve him.

David went down to Saul's house and knocked on the door. Ziba answered and almost fainted when he saw the king himself standing there. David asked him, if there was anyone left from the house of Saul that he could show his kindness to for his friend Jonathan's sake. Ziba answered David by telling him that there was someone left, Jonathan's son Mephibosheth who was now living in Lo-Debar.

Ziba went to inform them that King David had come to

the house of Saul looking for any surviving relatives. He informed the King that Mephibosheth was in Lo-Debar and now King David wanted to see him. Anger ripped through Mephibosheth's fear. Why did Ziba rat him out?!

Ziba was in charge of taking care of Mira-Baal's property. Mephibosheth couldn't take of his own property, crippled as he was. Ziba however, wanted the property for himself. That's why he ratted Mephibosheth out, so that David, the new king would assassinate him, and then all the property would belong to Ziba. Mephibosheth thought.

There was nothing Mephibosheth could do. His legs didn't work. He could not run. He could not fight. He could only face the end of his life with dignity and go see this King David face to face. Mephibosheth felt like he was cursed, because of his grandfather's disobedience everything went wrong for him.

At times he wished he'd never been born a prince, but there was no way of changing that. They placed Mephibosheth on the floor, by the steps of the throne where King David sat. Mephibosheth stretched out his hands and put his face to the ground, afraid to look at King David. He hoped the sword that was to end his life would fall quickly.

*"Don't be afraid,* King David said, *'for I will surely show you kindness for the sake of your father Jonathan. I will restore to you all the land that belonged to your grandfather Saul, and you will always eat at my table."*

Mephibosheth quickly put his face to the ground and said, *"Who am I that you should notice a dead dog like me?"* That was a befitting analogy. Whoever opposed David ended up dead anyway, like Goliath. To oppose David was to oppose God. As Mephibosheth waited face down, waited for the sword to cut through his body, waited for the curse to do its worst, nothing happened!

Not only did King David make Ziba Mephibosheth's servant but also all of Ziba's family. All that belonged to his grandfather Saul, now belonged to him. Mephibosheth was to be given a position of honor with King David at his dinner table.

Mira-Baal didn't understand why. That took a while. He found out King David and Jonathan, his father, had been very good friends before Jonathan was killed. He learned also that the two made a promise to each other in the sight of God: that if anything should happen to either one, the other would look out for his family. He also discovered something very special about David – David had God's love in his heart, and he wanted to show God's love and God's kindness to others – even to Mephibosheth.

It was God's love that brought him back to a position in the king's palace. It was the love of God that made him a prince again. He was part of the royal family. The Lord made the promise to his children that He would turn their curses into blessings. Mephibosheth, the Son of Shame discovered that – the day he met the love of God in King David.

If Mephibosheth had gotten away, he would've been killed. There would have been no one to keep the covenant with. God is a promise keeper. Sometimes He'll have to cripple you for a season and keep you in hiding so that the enemy can't find you. He'll keep you there until your *favor* show up! Just when you were about to give up, favor knocked on your door, and told destiny, go and bring 'em to me!

I'm here to encourage you, to let you know, every crisis is an opportunity. Whether you believe it or not, it's all working together for your good. 1 Peter 5:10, "But the God of all grace, who has called us unto His eternal glory by Christ Jesus, after that you have suffered a while, will restore, establish, strengthen, and settle you." There is an after this!

## The Word:

- 2 Samuel 4:4
- 2 Samuel 9
- 2 Samuel 16:1-4
- 2 Samuel 19:24-30
- 2 Samuel 21:7
- 1 Peter 5:10
- Jeremiah 30:17
- Isaiah 61:7
- Joel 2:25-26
- Job 42:10

- Isaiah 1:18
- 2 Corinthians 5:17
- Zechariah 9:12
- Jeremiah 17:14
- Ephesians 4:32
- Luke 6:36
- Colossians 3:12-14
- Proverbs 17:9
- Exodus 21:34
- Psalm 51:12
- Amos 9:14
- 2 Corinthians 13:9-11
- Galatians 6:1

## The Prayer:

"Father, we say thank You! You remember when others forget! When we were crippled by the vicissitudes of life, You didn't allow us to remain in a place of Lo-Debar. Instead You restored us to our rightful place in You.

We are truly grateful that You sent destiny to reclaim us, and the blood of Jesus to redeem us. Thank You, Kind Sir, that victory is our portion and because of that, we'll never be defeated! In Jesus' Name, we pray, Amen."

# WHEN LOVING YOU
# IS HURTING ME

What happens when you find yourself making foolish decisions all in the name of love? When you have extended yourself to others in so many ways, and it seems like the more you give, the more they take, and there is no true reciprocation of that which you have so generously provided?

What happens when you receive that knock on the door, after you promised yourself that the last time *was* the last time?

Now the person who holds your heart in their hand is standing on the doorsteps of your emotions. You can't quite say 'no' because the soul tie is so deep, that it seems that a very possible God can't seem to help you get out of this, what seems to be impossible situation.

We have all been there, in the place where we couldn't seem to *"measure up."* When misplaced love caused us, for a brief moment, to turn our backs on our confession and willingly take temptation by the hand, and say as the songstress Anita Baker puts it: *"Lead Me into Love."*

The question now becomes, *is this really love?* Is this the type of love God desires for me to have, or is this the only love I've ever known? Are my nights so long and lonely that I have to give myself away to be used and abused by anyone and everyone? Just to feel empty, abandoned and depleted. Just to hear those three empty words: *I Love You!*

True love causes you to cry tears of joy, not tears of pain, bitterness and sorrow. True love reaches beyond the satin sheets of fornication, masturbation and self-humiliation. Love – the *God* kind of love – will call just to say *"hello,"* without looking for a rendezvous.

What happens when loving you starts to hurt me? What happens when my dreams become nightmares because I shared my secrets with the wrong one? I become so impenetrable that even though physically I'm no longer chaste, my heart becomes so bitter, it becomes clasped.

What happens when loving *you* is hurting *me? I wake up!* I take a retrospective look within myself, to forgive myself, because I gave myself away, to someone who really didn't love me. I am no longer giddy nor beguiled. You took my heart and you raped it. Yeah, I trusted you, went on a date with you; and you took possession over that which you did not own, and when we were through, all you could do, is whisper in my ear, those same three empty words: I Love You.

That's it, I see! What you taught me wasn't love. It wasn't love at all. It was a manipulated attempt to destroy my soul. You taught me how to speak in tongues and feel ecstasy, that I was *nothing* if you weren't next to me. You took my power and revealed my mysteries, but when it was over, you wouldn't even speak to me.

I thought that my tears would fade away, with the promises of you'll be back someday. So when you called I jumped and I jumped. Paid your child support while I jumped and I jumped. Until one day, the bank called to say my account was overdrawn. The phone calls stopped, and the pain began again. Because you had me thinking that no matter what I say, what I believe or what I do, that I'd be *bankrupt* if I didn't have you.

But one day, I bumped into love, just when I thought I was going to die. True love stepped in, smiled and said, *"Let me introduce myself, I Am God, but my friends call me, The Most High!"*

After some time, getting to know God and removing the pains of my past, He taught me to look at you as a joker, which caused me to laugh. God taught me something that you never did. See, I was doing all of those things, but still, I couldn't live. I couldn't live because I was wrapped up in the perception of what love *should be*. That's when I realized that *loving you* was *hurting me!*

See, God taught me that: Love never gives up. Love cares more for others than for self. That love doesn't want what love doesn't have. That love doesn't have a big ego, or force itself on or take advantage of others.

That love isn't me first and flies off the handle. Love doesn't keep the scores on the sins of others. Love doesn't revel when others beg or plead. Love takes pleasure in truth and love puts up with *anything!* And by the way, *my* love trusts in God and always looks for the best. Love told me to never look back, to keep pressing ahead and that the love I now share – that love, will *never* end.

So thank you for the memories. Without you, I didn't know I could be this strong. And with heartfelt gratitude, I say... *"So long!"*

When dealing with love, we see that the misconception of love is always wrapped up in a give-and-take collaboration of two or more parties, which sometimes concludes with heartache, heartbreak and a pain that causes one to look at the other with walls of brick and mortar – daring the person on the opposite side to try to penetrate through. The alarm of one's past pain sends an alert to the heart that screams, *"Intruder alert!"*

That's because most have not understood what love is. What is love? You ask. The question should be: *"What is your definition of love?"* We can read self-help books about this controversial topic and look up as many definitions the dictionary has to offer. But until we experience the extremities of what love is to *us*, and decipher what it is *we* have gained and what it is *we* have lost while experimenting with this love thing, all *we* are, are infatuated beings.

Many are infatuated with the thought of being in love. So it is with our relationship with God. Do we really love Him as we say we do or are we just infatuated with Him?

John 3:16 states, *"For God so greatly loved and dearly prized the world that He [even] gave up His only begotten (unique) Son, so that whoever believes in (trusts in, clings to, relies on) Him shall not perish (come to destruction, be lost) but have eternal (everlasting) life."*

That love has to do with sacrificial love. I gave of myself so you could have. I'm not only looking at the *price* of the item that was purchased, but I'm looking at the lasting *investment* of that which has just been purchased. Therefore, infatuation doesn't look at the overall purpose of the relationship. Infatuation lives and loves in the moment.

Have you ever loved and individual and found out that the person never loved you the way you loved them? Not even a tittle of love was shown. You realized that you were exhausting your time and energy in a person that didn't care if you existed or not.

Imagine how God feels. He became flesh and blood, and moved into the neighborhood. We saw the glory with our own eyes, the one-of-a-king glory, like Father, like Son. Generous inside and out, true from start to finish. Still at the end of the day, we ended up rejecting the love He has for us.

We at times only want a fabricated relationship with God based on momentary needs. We call him up like He's Santa Claus, with demands of what we need Him to do for us. But even Santa had a limit. Even *he knew* if you were *naughty or nice*. God, unlike Santa, *knows all things*, whether *naughty or nice*, and that is what makes God Omniscient.

What I love about God is that in spite of ourselves, our hidden agendas and selfish motives, He [God] still looked beyond our faults, saw our needs, pushed past our sins, saw the blood of Jesus, heard our cries, delivered us from pits, and elevated us to palaces. He still stays, even though He's caught us sleeping with the enemy. He loved us enough to forgive us, keep our secrets, save our souls, walk us down the aisle and make us His bride, His church.

Because we compare God's love with man's love, we sometimes miss the opportunity through grace to accept that He really does love us as we are.

Well, someone may ask, *"What is grace?"* Grace, my friend, is God's unmerited favor. It is kindness from God that we don't deserve. There is nothing we have done, nor can ever do, to earn this favor. It is a gift from God.

God's kind of love is unconditional. He'll take you: new, old, refurbished, undone, manufactured, warranty or not. He'll love you fat, skinny, blemished or beautiful. Because we've been so conditioned to what we've learned that love is, we in turn do what we believe love does. So, let me help you by telling you what love *isn't...*

If you speak with human eloquence and angelic ecstasy but don't love, you are nothing but the creaking of a rusty gate. If you speak God's word with power, revealing all His mysteries and making everything plain as day, and if you have faith that says to a mountain, "Jump," and it jumps, but you don't love, you are nothing. If you give everything you own to the poor and even go to the stake to be burned as a martyr, but you don't love, you've gotten nowhere. So no matter what you say, what you believe and, or what you do, you are *bankrupt* without love!

Now you may ask me, *"What is love?"* Love endures long *and* is patient *and* kind; love never is envious *nor* boils over with jealousy. Love is *not* boastful or vainglorious, does not display itself haughtily. Love is not conceited (arrogant and inflated with pride). Love (God's love in us) does not insist on its own rights *or* its own way, for it is not self-seeking; it is not touchy *or* fretful *or* resentful; it takes *no* account of the evil done to it [it pays no attention to a suffered wrong]. It does not rejoice at injustice *and* unrighteousness, but rejoices when right *and* truth prevail.

Love bears up under anything *and* everything that comes and is ever ready to believe the best of every person. It hopes are fadeless under all circumstances, and it endures everything [without weakening]. Love never fails [never fades out or becomes obsolete or comes to an end].

When we have God's love in our heart, we can send a postcard to our heartbreakers and sign it:

Love,
*"I got my heart back!"*

God's love is a pure love. It has no agenda. It has no demands. All He requires of you, is to love Him back. God is a gentleman. He loves you so much until His ultimate goal is to heal your broken heart. He doesn't want you to cover up your wounds with religion. He actually wants to heal your wounds with *relationship.*

Walk with me over to the book of John, Chapter 4. Let's take a look at the woman at the well. He came into Sychar, a Samaritan village that bordered the field Jacob had given his son Joseph. Jacob's well was still there. Jesus, worn out by his trip, sat down at the well. It was noon.

A woman, a Samaritan, came to draw water. Jesus said, *"Would you give me a drink of water?"* (His disciples had gone to the village to buy food for lunch). The Samaritan woman, taken aback, asked, *"How come you, a Jew, are asking me, a Samaritan woman, for a drink?"* (Jews in those days wouldn't be caught dead talking to Samaritans).

Jesus answered, *"If you knew the generosity of God and who I am, you would be asking me for a drink, and I would give you fresh, living water."*

The woman said, *"Sir, you don't even have a bucket to draw with, and this well is deep. So how are you going to get this living water? Are you a better man than our ancestor Jacob, who dug this well and drank from it, he and his sons and livestock, and passed it down to us?"*

Jesus said, *"Everyone who drinks this water will get thirsty again and again. Anyone who drinks the water I give will never thirst – not ever. The water I give will be an artesian spring within, gushing fountains of endless life."*

The woman said, *"Sir, give me this water so I won't ever get thirsty, won't ever have to come back to this well again!" He said, "Go call your husband and then come back."*

*"I have no husband,"* she said.

"That is nicely put: 'I have no husband.' You've had five husbands, and the man you're living with now isn't even your husband. You spoke the truth there, sure enough."

"Oh so you're a prophet! Well, then tell me this: Our ancestors worshiped God at this mountain, but you Jews insist that Jerusalem is the only place for worship, right?"

"Believe me, woman, the time is coming when you Samaritans will worship the Father neither here at this mountain nor there in Jerusalem. You worship guessing in the dark; we Jews worship in the clear light of day. God's way of salvation is made available through the Jews. But the time is coming – it has, in fact come – when what you're called will not matter and where you go to worship will not matter.

"It's who you are and the way you live that count before God. Your worship must engage your spirit in the pursuit of truth. That's the kind of people the Father is out looking for: those who are simply and honestly themselves before Him in their worship. God is sheer being itself – Spirit. Those who worship Him must do it out of their very being, their spirits, their true selves, in adoration."

The woman said, "I don't know about that. I do know that the Messiah is coming. When He arrives, we'll get the whole story."

"I am He," said Jesus. "You don't have to wait any longer or look any further."

Just then His disciples came back. They were shocked. They couldn't believe He was talking to *that* kind of woman. No one said what they were all thinking, but their faces showed it.

The woman took the hint and left. In her confusion she left her water pot. Back in the village she told the people, "Come see a man who knew all about the things I did, who knows me inside and out. Do you think this could be the Messiah?" And they went out to see for themselves.

Right there in Samaria under the shade of a well, among a rejected people in the face of a blackballed, cast-down, downtrodden, excluded, ostracized woman, Jesus disrobed His identity. It wasn't before a great crowd of people; He didn't call for a news conference and say 'I am the Messiah!' No, right there at the well, He became intimate with her spirit so that He could reach her soul.

He spoke to her just enough to get her attention. He entertained her just enough to gain her trust. He did this without badgering her of her past sins or condemning her for the present ones. With *love* He spoke to her past and introduced her to her future. And, with just a cup, a well and a conversation, she understood that not only could she be free from the dominion and power of sin but that she could worship at the well if she wanted to. She didn't need permission; all she needed was to be persuaded.

Many of the Samaritans from that village committed themselves to Him because of the woman's witness: *"He knew all about the things I did. He knows me inside and out!"* They asked Him to stay on, so Jesus stayed two days. A lot more people entrusted their lives to Him when they heard what He had to say. They said to the woman, *"We're no longing taking this on your say-so. We've heard it for ourselves and know it for sure. He's the Savior of the world!"*

It was His *love* for her that said, *I want you.* You had five husbands and the one waiting for you to come back as we speak don't even belong to you, *but I want you!* I want you just as you are! Faults and all, I want you! Failures, yeah, you've had them, who hasn't? I still want you!

And that is what the Lord is saying to us today, I want you just the way you are, disrobe yourself of your religious beliefs, come and let us reason together. I want to give you a drink of my *love* potion; I want to give you some of this *living* water. Once you've tasted of my goodness, you'll trust me, and it'll bless you! It's guaranteed, imported from the heavens. I promise you, you'll never thirst again.

Go home, evict the intruder out of your heart. I, Jesus am standing here today, knocking on the doors of your heart, asking you to let me in. The day you hear my voice, please don't harden your heart. I want to go on a date with you. I want to sup with you. Let *me* be your first husband!

I know you're learning how to trust again, how to love again. I'll be gentle with you. I won't rush a thing. Give me your heart, place it in my hands. Yeah, that's it! That's true love that you're feeling! Here, let me be your handkerchief, as a matter of fact, let me take your tears and bottle them up for you. You won't cry because someone has hurt you ever again, no, not like before. I will wipe all your tears away!

## The Word:

- John 3:16
- John 4:1-4
- Psalm 34:8
- 1 Corinthians 13
- Ephesians 2:8
- Luke 6:31
- Romans 12:9
- Romans 13:10
- 1 John 4:7, 18-9
- Colossians 3:14
- Proverbs 17:17
- 1 John 3:16-18
- Song of Solomon 8:4-8
- Exodus 14:14

## The Prayer:

"Father, I thank You for Your love. I thank You for Your grace, Your unmerited favor. Where would I be without it? I'd be lost like a ship without a sail! Like the woman at the well, You came and changed me, saved me and forgave me, and took me as I was. I am eternally satisfied with You and in You. In Jesus' Name, I pray, Amen."

# SINGING THE BLUES
# IN TUNE UNTIL
# THE SUN COMES UP

Remember the popular English nursery rhyme that went like this, *"Rain, Rain, go away, come again another day?"* Many of us can recall that nursery rhyme at some point in time in our life.

Especially on those days when it was raining and we longed to be outdoors enjoying the day. But the forecast and shadows of clouds forced us to remain indoors, tucked away from the droplets of rain and the sometimes noisome thunder that caused us to shiver from its sound.

Yet, through all of that, we still wished for the rain to stop, the sun to shine and, if we were lucky a glimpse of rainbow, as a sign to let us know that the rain had ceased its fall. It was now safe for us to come out of our hiding place and go outside to play.

As children and, to be honest, as adults, we never thought about rain or its purpose. All we knew was the presence of rain threatened to inconvenience our plans for the day. Rain would at times catch us off guard. There we would be, vulnerable to the rain, without shelter, without umbrellas, raincoats or rain boots.

And even though we were caught in the rain, there was

absolutely nothing we could do about it; except seek shelter, stand still and wait for the passing storm to move on, and then try resume our day as best we could.

Billie Holiday sang a song called *"Stormy Weather,"* written in 1933 by Harold Arlen and Ted Koehler. However, Ethel Waters sang it first, at the Cotton Club, a then-popular night club in New York City's Harlem.

The song sings of the disappointment of how she and her man weren't together, due to there being no sun in the sky, and the fact that it kept raining all the time. She felt blue, grim and sad, because she couldn't have who she wanted and she couldn't be where she needed, because the weather just never seemed to be in her favor.

She sang of how her life was bare, gloomy and filled with misery. How she was weary and couldn't get herself together. She also sang of being afraid that her old rocking chair would get her. She'd pray that the Lord above would just let her walk in the sun just once more.

But what Miss Billie Holiday didn't know while singing about stormy weather, was that eventually the storm would end, and the weather would change. Once the sun shone, what she was missing, she probably really didn't miss at all.

What would come springing up from the ground would be beautiful and new, pleasant and budding, fragrant and lovely, promising and plentiful.

In life, regardless of who you are, where you've been or what you know, you will experience a rainy day. Like Miss Holiday, you too will sing the *why today, must it rain blues.* No one is exempt from cloudy days or misty nights. We all will have to say like the old English nursery rhyme, *"Rain, Rain, go away, come again another day!"* But, do we really know what we're saying when we recite that nursery rhyme?

Remember, no one really knows when it will rain. Meteorologists aren't always accurate with their forecasts. What if I told you that your forecast has changed and that life as you've known it isn't going to end up the way you expected? What if I told you that the rainy days that you're going through right now serve a purpose, and what you are experiencing, though it may be an inconvenience now, in the long run, is going to serve a major purpose?

Don't put away those umbrellas just yet. Find you a compact umbrella, stick it in your bag or in the trunk of your car. You may need it today, or you may not. Just in case, get it and keep it someplace handy.

In the 23rd book of the bible known as Isaiah, we see this Major Prophet whose name means Jehovah is Salvation, speak about rain throughout this miniature bible of sixty-six chapters. Isaiah 55:10 starts off with a prophecy. He says:

*"For as the rain and snow come down from the heavens, and return not there again, but water the earth and make it bring forth and sprout, that it may give seed to the sower and bread to the eater..."*

He then smoothed it over with a prophecy form verses 11-13 by saying: *"So shall My word be that goes forth out of My mouth: it shall not return to Me void [without producing any effect, useless], but it shall accomplish that which I please and purpose, and it shall prosper in the thing for which I sent it.*

*"For you shall go out [from the spiritual exile caused by sin and evil into the homeland] with joy and be led forth [by your Leader, the Lord Himself, and His word] with peace; the mountains and the hills shall break forth before you into singing, and all the trees of the field shall clap their hands.*

*"Instead of the thorn shall come up the cypress tree, and instead of the brier shall come up the myrtle tree; and it shall be to the Lord for a name of renown, for an everlasting sign [of jubilant exaltation] and memorial [to His praise], which shall not be cut off."*

In other words, what He is saying is that the purpose of the rain is to bring forth. Sometimes rain *is* good for you because in the long run, its purpose will produce on your behalf. That's why the Lord told Isaiah to prophesy and promise us that not only will it produce seed to those of us that sow, but that the seed would produce bread that will supply food for us to live on.

I want to encourage you and let you know that the next time your life seems a little cloudy and it looks as if the forecast calls for rain, don't be disturbed by the inconvenience, because God is saying to us whenever we see rain, we can expect a Word!

He likens the rain to His word. Every time it rains, God is saying, I am speaking to your situation! Change your song! This rain isn't fruitless, useless and ineffective. No ma'am, no Sir. This word brings forth, and it produces!

The untimeliness of rain, acts in the timeliness of God. It saturates the ground and maturates the seed. God allows the vexation and peril of such inconvenience to give you newness. To wash away the hindrances of your present state, to change the dial on your radio from doom and gloom, to joy with a new song that'll have you singing along and clapping your hands.

God pulls water up out of the sea, distills it, and fills up His rain-cloud cisterns. Then the skies open up and pour out soaking showers on everyone. Does anyone have the slightest idea how this happens? How He arranges the clouds? How He speaks in thunder? Just look at the lightning, His sky-filling light show, illuminating the dark depths of sea! These are the symbols of His Sovereignty, His generosity, His loving care.

He hurls arrows of light, taking sure to and accurate aim. The High God roars in thunder, angry against evil.

You won't see your garden as just a garden, but you'll begin to see all that was planted come into full bloom! They that sow in tears will reap in joy; your tears will pay off. All those times you cried in the dark, under the covers, hiding from the thunder, shivering from the storms of life, afraid that the rocking chair that was supposed to bring you comfort, would imprison you with the fear of being alone and lonely.

No need to feel alone any longer or be afraid of the clapping of the thunder. It's only the Lord speaking through the clouds. I was just like you, whenever this happened, my heart stopped – I was thunderstruck. I couldn't catch my breath. I listened to it! I listened to His thunder, the rolling, rumbling thunder of His voice.

He let loose His lightning from horizon to horizon, lighting up the earth from pole to pole. In their wake, the thunder echoes His voice, powerful and majestic.

He lets out all the stops. He holds nothing back. No one can mistake that voice – His word thundering so wondrously, His mighty acts staggering our understanding.

He orders the snow, *'Blanket the earth!'* and the rain, *'Soak the whole countryside!'* No one can escape the weather – it's there. And no one can escape God's breath from God. Wild animals take shelter, crawling into their dens, when blizzards roar out of the north and freezing rain crusts the land.

It's God's breath that forms the ice; it's God's breath that turns lakes and rivers solid. And yes, it's God who fills clouds with rainwater and hurls lightning from them every which way. He puts them through their paces – first this way, then that – commands them to do what He says all over the world. Whether for discipline or grace or extravagant love, He makes sure they make their mark.

Your tears have watered your rain garden and joy has sprung up a well within your soul! Know that the rain you were experiencing wasn't only for you but also those around you. You are God's very own rain garden. A rain garden is a planted depression that allows the overflow of rainwater to turn off from impervious areas. It's designed for specific soils and climates.

The purpose of a rain garden is to improve water quality in nearby bodies of water. Also, through the process of transpiration, rain garden plants return water vapors to the atmosphere, covering all the possible elements that can be used to capture, channel, divert, and make the most of the natural rain and snow that falls.

The depression you were in only prepared you to catch the overflow! You were designed to survive specific trials and tribulations; in other words, no matter what circumstances to you find yourself in – in life, you were destined to survive it. Not *only* survive it, but also to be an atmosphere changer!

God chose you because He could trust you. Knowing that you would vigorously hold on to what it is He'd given you. While going through the pathway of life, turning others to Him from different directions, making the most out of what it is He gave you.

Know that the favor of God is with you and that you can put away your Billie Holiday collection and bring out your Clark Sisters anthology. Place the volume of your life on full blast as you sing along with Jacky, Denise, Twinkie, Dorinda and Karen as they sing to Lord in perfect harmony, *"You Brought the Sunshine!"*

Unlike Billie, you won't be singing about just *any* man, you'll be singing about Jesus! You can rest assured, knowing that when it rains again, and it will – there may be a hint of fog, but that's okay! If you're traveling, pull to the side of the road. If you're in the house, sit by a window – God is up to something!

Whenever FOG appears it's to let you know that God's working behind the scenes. He's working on those things that you cannot see. It is also letting you know that once the FOG lifts, the curtains of your life will too be lifted and when they do, you'll be taking center stage. What's been in the making behind the scenes all this time is about to be revealed! Till then, enjoy the rain!

| The Word: |
|---|

- Job 36:27-33
- Job 37:6
- Job 28:26
- Psalm 68:8
- Jeremiah 10:13
- Isaiah 55:10-13
- Philippians 4:8
- Deuteronomy 31:8
- Psalm 40:1-3
- Psalm 34:17
- 1 Peter 5:7
- 2 Corinthians 1:3-4

- 1 Peter 4:12-13
- Isaiah 45:8
- Isaiah 4:6
- Hebrews 6:7
- Jeremiah 51:16
- Psalm 135:7

## The Prayer:

"Father, in the Name of Jesus, I come to thank You for the rain. You told me that whenever I see rain to expect a word!

Father, thank You that the rain in my life serves a purpose! Thank You that every cloudy day brings a silver lining. Thank You for speaking a word of purpose and bringing the sunshine in my life. You are great and You are God!

You brought the Sunshine in my life. Since that I have found Christ, there has been such a change in my life! In Jesus' Name. Amen."

# POWERFUL, PRIDEFUL
# AND PITIFUL

I'm a leader! I'm being promoted! After all this time, God has given me the go ahead to become the next greatest in the kingdom and I'm excited about it!

Prophecy is finally being fulfilled and I'm ecstatic! Here, take that, devil! And to all of you who said I'd never be, look at me now! I'm in control, now what!

No. Really, *now what?* That shouldn't be a rhetorical question. That should be a rhetorical response; because at the end of the day, the party is over and yes, you're in the reigning princess, the pious king, the wonderful choice, the people's choice, and yes, maybe even God's choice for the people. However, remember that – that's all you are – no more and no less.

Ever met someone who thought that they were so wonderful that even the sun dimmed and bowed out when *they* woke up in the morning? So full of their own glory that even God – the One that created them – called them and yes, even gave them their position – couldn't even convince them that even the sun has to go down at evening tide.

Arrogance and pride are two lethal doses that, when used separately, can cause a slow death. But when consumed together, they can become so toxic that once digested they will cause a detrimental destruction that the individuals who drink it can't even be recognized among their demise.

Power, though it is a great thing, can be a very dangerous tool when in the wrong hands. Especially, when the person to whom the power has been given is so far gone, intoxicated within his or her own self-aggrandizement, that reality is no longer reality but delusions of grandeur.

He or she is so engulfed in making themselves seem so much more than they really are, that they become boastful and egotistical, almost menacing. Self-praised, self-glorified and all those who are attached to them, in whatever capacity, must worship them in a likewise manner. If not, the individuals who refuses to become bewitched find themselves the target.

I remember as I was maturing in the things of God, I found myself becoming a victim of such people. Everything and everyone around them was to be reminded of how great *they* were. If it wasn't for God bringing *them* into our lives, *we* wouldn't be anything. *We* ought to be grateful for what it is *they* represented to *us*. If *we* were to not go along with how *important* these persons wanted *us* to believe *they* were, God had this great *doom* and *wrath* that would be heading our way to destroy us.

Apparently, I never went along with this plan and soon I became shunned and treated as if I were an enemy to that particular fellowship of *"believers."* And, because I would not go to the extremities that others would to appease the ego of these people, I was labeled, even blackballed.

Remember the story of Humpty Dumpty? As a child most, if not all, of you read the popular children's nursery rhyme:

> *"Humpty Dumpty sat on a wall,*
> *Humpty Dumpty had a great fall.*
> *All the king's horses and all the king's men*
> *Couldn't put Humpty together again."*

So was the case of King Ahab and his oh-so wonderful, and I say this sarcastically – *wife,* the infamous, Queen Jezebel. Naboth the Jezreelite had a vineyard next to the palace of King Ahab of Samaria. The king asked Naboth for the vineyard that he may have it for a vegetable garden for it was near, next to his house. And in exchange for the garden the king was willing to give Naboth a better vineyard or money for its worth.

And Naboth said to Ahab, *"The Lord forbids that I should give the inheritance of my fathers to you!"* So Ahab went into his house sullen and displeased. He lay down on his bed, and turned away his face, and would eat no food.

Then Jezebel his wife said to him, *"You now exercise authority over Israel! Arise and eat food, and let your heart be cheerful; I will give you the vineyard of Naboth the Jezreelite."*

So Jezebel wrote a letter in Ahab's name, sealed it with his seal and sent the letter to the elders and nobles who were dwelling in the city with Naboth. And she wrote in the letter saying:

*"Proclaim a fast, and seat Naboth with high honor among the people, and seat two men, scoundrels, before him, to bear witness against him saying, 'You have blasphemed God and the King!' Then take him out, and stone him, that he may die."*

The men of the city, the elders and nobles did as Jezebel had sent them, as it was written in the letter which she had sent them. When Jezebel was told of Naboth's death she said to Ahab, *"Arise, and take possession of the vineyard of Naboth the Jezreelite which he refuses to give you for money; for Naboth is dead."*

So it was when Ahab heard that Naboth was dead that Ahab got up, and went down to take possession of the vineyard. Then the word of the Lord came to Elijah the Tishbite.

*"You shall speak to Ahab, saying, thus says the Lord: "Have you murdered and also taken possession? Thus says the Lord: 'In the place where the dogs licked the blood of Naboth, dogs shall lick your blood, even yours."*

And concerning Jezebel the Lord also spoke saying, *"The dogs shall eat Jezebel by the wall of Jezreel."*

When Humpty Dumpty sat on the wall, he sat on a wall of pride. The problem with Humpty Dumpty was, even though he was given permission to be on the wall, he didn't properly secure himself for the height of the position to which he would hold. Normally, when someone is sitting or standing in a lofty place, he or she is supported by railings and harnesses that would prevent them from falling.

In the bible, when an individual was high in position, as far as sitting on a wall, it was only because God had called them to be a watchman on the wall. Such was the case of the prophet Ezekiel, whose job was warning when a destroying army was approaching. Ezekiel was called to this ministry in Chapter 3 and reinforced in Chapter 33. But he was not reliant on the predictions of the meteorologists, but rather the Lord who speaks and warns of the approaching storm.

The reason why Humpty Dumpty fell was that, as the word of the Lord states in Proverbs 16:18, *"Pride goes before destruction, a haughty spirit before a fall."* Humpty's fall came after being warned, I'm sure. Not only did he fall and was broken into so many pieces; but even the king's horses and king's men couldn't put him back together again. The bible states in Jeremiah 30:12, *"Your hurt is incurable, and your wound is grievous."*

He was so broken until he couldn't even be healed. God even said to Jeremiah, "Stop praying for these people!" Whenever you become stubborn and continue to do it *your* way, and treat God's people any kind of way, *God* will deal with you.

When leaders are in positions of this magnitude, they must be careful not to take advantage of others, or manipulate others as to forcibly take that which rightfully belongs to them. They must remember that they are called to minister to those to whom they have been assigned. They must also be careful not to manipulate their flock into thinking, that the flock is required to serve according to their needs only, and then assess the flock's faithfulness to God based upon how well the flock serves them.

In 1 Kings 17, we see the widow of Zarephath, a woman who, like many of us, was going through a very difficult time in her life. As we look at her story, we find that the land she is in has not had rain for some time. Because of the drought, there is no water, no crops, and no food. She is preparing for her and her son to die.

However, the Lord instructs the prophet Elijah to go down to Zarephath and tells him that his needs will be supplied by a widow there. In obedience, Elijah does as the Lord tells him. As Elijah expected, he is met by the widow the Lord told him about. Elijah knew that the Lord promised food from this widow, so he asks her for water and a piece of bread.

The widow expects that she and her son will die of starvation. She knows her situation and her common sense tells her what the eventual outcome will be. God prepared the widow woman for the prophet Elijah, before he arrived at the place of divine purpose and provision. He did not put on a prophet's cape and demand that she bless him in order to access the blessings the righteous already have through covenant.

He came on behalf of the Lord to *be* a blessing, not to *take* a blessing, or *manipulate* her out of a blessing. Neither did he come to *kill* her or her son who appeared to be dying from desperation, to get what it is the *Lord* already had prepared for *all of them!*

He did not *approach* her as to be her knight in shining armor. He approached her for what he was, a mouthpiece of God. He wasn't arrogant or prideful as Humpty Dumpty had been, neither was he menacing or malicious as Ahab and Jezebel. But with humility, he assessed the situation and advised her that *if* she would obey *God*, she and her son would live.

The difference between someone living in a penthouse and others living in the projects can be the choices one makes. As children of God we have to be careful that we don't confuse the congregants by telling them that we have obtained more than them because God favored us about the rest. That's a lie from the pit of hell. We will cause people's faith to waiver. People have sat in church for years thinking God has special picks. He (God) does not have special picks. We are all called and assigned to different tasks. That's it and that's all.

To say otherwise is wizardry and witchcraft, when we manipulate the scriptures to make people think we are something that we are not. Encourage the people by preaching the gospel through and through – Romans 10:17, says, *"So then faith cometh by hearing and hearing by the word of God."* If we would just learn to give people God and not our opinions, we would see how many lives could be changed.

Jezebel had no right to kill Naboth, simply because the *"king"* wanted something that rightfully, did not belong to him. Be careful of the people who are willing to kill you in order to take what is yours. A lot of people have died spiritually because they allowed another to disinherit them.

Make sure that you know, regardless of the plot that is out to destroy you, label you or even blacklist you, that what you have, God gave it to you and no one can take it away – not even Jezebel and Ahab.

Remain faithful, you don't have to be like Humpty Dumpty and have a dreadful end. Do what Apostle Paul commanded when he said: *"For by the grace given me I say to every one of you: Do not think yourself more highly than you ought, but rather think of yourself with sober judgment, in accordance with the measure of faith God has given you."* And in the same way, *"Let your light shine before men, that they may see your good deeds and praise your Father in heaven."*

## The Word:

- Matthew 5:15
- Romans 12:3
- 1 Kings 17
- 1 Kings 21
- Proverbs 16:18
- 1 Peter 5:6
- 1 John 2:16
- Leviticus 26:19
- Obadiah 1:3
- 2 Chronicles 26:16

- Psalm 10:4
- Proverbs 11:2
- Galatians 6:4
- Job 40:11
- James 4:10

## The Prayer:

"Father, in the Name of Jesus I pray that You keep me from a haughty spirit. I pray that in everything that You allow me to do, that all glory goes back to You! Break this spirit of pride and rebellion, and cause humility to cover my heart like a blanket. In Jesus' Name, I pray. Amen."

# YOU'RE COMING OUT

Cry me a river, why don't you! Ever wanted to scream that to someone at the top of your lungs? You almost didn't want to ask them how their day was going or better yet, how the family was.

You dreaded walking into that person altogether because you knew that when you did, you would be forced to exchange pleasantries, and that all too familiar question would be asked. It cannot be avoided and there is absolutely no way around it.

As the person sits patiently, waiting for you to ask, you look at the clock on the wall ahead of you so hard, you can actually hear the second hand tick away into minutes. Just when you thought you could avoid the golden question, out of your mouth comes those three dooming words, *how are you?*

Normally when someone asks you, *how are you?* they really don't care for an actual response, but because it is the right thing to ask immediately after saying hello they ask anyhow. And most people ask because they were taught that it would be considered rude not to.

But, are we to care? Are we to really ask the age-old question and really *wait* for a response? Should we really be concerned about how another individual is faring? Or should we just be pleasant enough to smile and walk away quickly before they can respond?

I mean, why ask the question if you really don't care? Why appear to be empathetic when you're really not? You may ask the question, should we be that concerned? The answer would simply be, yes.

From the beginning of time, God wanted us to care for one for another. He had left the example in Cain and Abel. I know we've read the story or heard it preached in times past. But what God was exemplifying to us is the ability to empathize one with another and to really help each other out.

Adam and Eve's sons, Cain the farmer and Abel the shepherd – though like most siblings who didn't always get along – loved each other very much. Adam and Eve disobeyed God prior to getting kicked out of the Garden of Eden. They were trying to get things right with God. So God, being merciful and true, required of them a sacrifice.

Adam and Eve passed on this request to their children to do likewise. Abel was very concerned that his sacrifice be special unto God. He chose his first and finest lamb and offered it to the Lord. It was hard for Abel to give up his most beloved animal, but it was important to him to try his best to obey God.

Cain thought his little brother was a bit featherbrained for giving up his best lamb. *"Good grief,"* he thought. *"We need that Lamb, God doesn't. I'm sure He'd be happy with whatever it is we can sacrifice. What does God need with a lamb anyway! I'm a farmer and thought I've had a great year from my wheat crop – I can't use it all, so why don't I just burn some of the extras, that way, I won't be wasting any."*

As a result, when God accepted Abel's sacrifice and rejected Cain's, Cain became jealous and killed his brother. He felt as if God loved Abel more, but that was not the case. God was giving Cain another opportunity to get it right by telling him sin lied at the door. But Cain was adamant to do things his way.

Cain *wasn't* empathetic enough to what the request was. It was all about how *he* felt and what *he* wanted. So instead of opening up his heart to receive what the Lord required, he took his anger out on an innocent – his own brother. He demonstrated his lack of empathy when the Lord asked Cain the now infamous question, *"Cain, where is your brother?"*

Cain replied, *"I don't know! Am I my brother's keeper?"*

When someone is empathetic, that mean's he or she has the ability to share another's emotions and feelings. The apostle Peter counseled Christians to have *"compassion for one another; love as brothers, be tenderhearted, be courteous,"* as spoken in 1 Peter 3:8.

We are to be concerned with one another. The apostle Paul recommended similar sentiments when he exhorted fellow Christians to *"rejoice with those who rejoice, and weep with those who weep,"* in Romans 12:15.

So we *are* our brother's keeper. We were created to bear

each other's burdens and to love each other unconditionally. To care when another cries, to take in one who has no place to sleep, to clothe one who has no linen and to feed the hungry. Within every one of us there is a conviction of grace that looks beyond ourselves to make sure that we care enough to consider the poor, the poor in heart, in spirit, to cheer others with a heavy heart, to look beyond ourselves sometimes and to care for others as we would ourselves.

Compassion, sympathy and empathy all have to do with passion (feeling) for another person, because you identify with his or her suffering. True empathy adds the expression of those feelings. Though we are aware of this and intend to love one another, we often overlook opportunities to relieve other's pain. That could be because we are not aware of other's needs.

There are four words in the Greek language for love. Each has a different connotation such as a loving nature, passionate love, or feelings of love rooted in pleasure or preciousness. *"Agapan"* and *"Philein"* are two of the words for love that are discussed.

Philein is intended to convey something different than a love born of preciousness *(Agapan)*. The concepts of intrinsic inner goodness, brotherly love, friendship, hospitality, "from the same womb," and love for mankind all have roots stemming from "Philein," and so does the word *"courteous."*

Courteous, 1 Peter 3:8 is from a word made up of Philein and a Greek word speaking of *"the faculty of perceiving and judging."* The courtesy spoken of here is that *rare and beautiful combination of friendliness and tactful and delicate sense of perception and judgment.*

It was John who said: *"But whoever has this world's goods, and sees his brothers in need, and shuts up his heart from him, how does the love of God abide in him?"* 1 John 3:17. We know that as Christians we are commanded to love our neighbor and to have intense love for one another, according to Matthew 22:39 and 1 Peter 4:8.

The Psalmist, King David, declared in Psalms 56:8, *"You know my wanderings; Put my tears into your bottle; Are they not in your book?"* Oh how comforting it is to know that even God records all of our tears as we struggle in our lives.

That's why whenever you make everything about *'YOU,"* it becomes *"I" dolatry!* When you do things, do not let selfishness or pride become your guide. Instead, be humble and give more honors to others than to yourselves. Do not be interested in *YOUR OWN* life, but be interested in the lives of *OTHERS!*

Even Jesus was cognizant and delicate to the needs and feelings of others. When reading, we see in Luke 7:11-16 that Jesus went to the village of Nain and His disciples were with him, along with quite a large crowd. As they approached the village gate, they met a funeral procession – a woman's only son was being carried out for burial. And the mother was a widow.

When Jesus saw her, his heart broke. He said to her, *"Don't cry."* Then he went over and touched the coffin. The pallbearers stopped. Jesus said, *"Young man, I tell you: Get up."* The dead son sat up and began talking. Jesus presented him to his mother. They all realized they were in a place of holy mystery that God was at work among them. They were quietly worshipful – and then noisily grateful – calling out among themselves, *"God is back, looking to the needs of his people!"*

All through the scriptures we find reasons why we should care for one another. In the book of 2 Corinthians, Paul explains the purpose of tribulation and affliction: it is so we can then feel for, and comfort others in their tribulations.

He states: *"Blessed be the God and Father of our Lord Jesus Christ, the Father of mercies and God of all comfort, who comforts us in all our tribulation that we may be able to comfort those who are in any trouble, with the comfort which we ourselves are comforted by God."*

The ultimate though, as usual, is Jesus Christ. According to the Hebraic writer who so eloquently put it like this: *"For we have not an high priest which cannot be touched with the feeling of our infirmities, but was in all points tempted like we are, yet without sin."*

He goes on to encourage us to *mourn* with those who are mourning, and to *rejoice* with those who are rejoicing, and *empathize* with those around us. Through this we will become better friends, brothers, sisters, helpmates, siblings, and parents. Even if you find that duty sends you into a place of leadership, let your heart feel the afflictions and distresses of everyone you have leadership over.

Remember when Jesus' good friend Lazarus died? When Lazarus was ill, they called Jesus, asking Him to come and heal Lazarus. But Jesus waited. After a couple of days, He told His disciples He was going to Bethany. Now Bethany was only two miles from Jerusalem. When Jesus arrived, Martha met Him on the road. She told Jesus Lazarus wouldn't have died if He had come sooner.

But she also added that she still believed the Father would do anything Jesus asked of Him. Her faith was very strong. Jesus said Lazarus would live again. Martha replied that she knew he would rise again on the last day. Jesus answered, *"I am the resurrection and the life. Those who believe in me, even though they die, will live, and everyone who lives and believes in me will never die. Do you believe this?"*

Martha said, *yes.* She believed Jesus was the Messiah.

Then Martha went back and sent Mary to Jesus. She, also, told Jesus that Lazarus would not have died if He had come sooner. The other Jews gathered around wondered why this great healer didn't heal His good friend. Jesus was greatly upset until He cried. He then asked to be shown where Lazarus lay. He told them to take away the big stone that blocked the tomb. Martha protested that it was too late; the body would be decaying already.

But Jesus reminded her of the glory of God. Jesus thanked the Lord for answering His prayer, so that the crowd would believe God sent Him. And He cried with a loud voice, *"Lazarus come out!"* And Lazarus came out of the tomb, still wrapped in burial cloths.

At times, you and I will become that handkerchief; that shoulder to cry on, that listening ear. At times you and I will be that voice coaxing someone from out of their grave clothes and into their fine linens. We never know what it is someone else may be going through or if we will be the tool that God will use to encourage them.

So, the next time you see a person who may be having a bad day, don't be afraid to ask them how they're doing. Don't be so quick to walk away or ignore their pain. As they lament and pour out their heart, be prayerful and sensitive. Encourage them as David did, when he wrote Psalm 30:5... *"Weeping may endure for a night, but joy comes in the morning."*

Just as Jesus cared for Martha, Mary, and Lazarus, He cares or you. His love is wide and long, high and deep – it never ends.

| The Word: |
| --- |

- 2 Corinthians 1:3-4
- Hebrews 4:15
- 1 John 3:17
- Luke 7:11-16

- 1 Peter 3:8
- Galatians 6:2
- Psalm 82:1-8
- Hebrews 3:12-15
- Colossians 3:9-10
- Genesis 4:8-10
- Genesis 4:1-26

## The Prayer:

"Father, I thank You for giving me the discernment to know what my brothers and sisters are going through, and for making me sensitive to another's needs other than my own. I am my brother's and sister's keeper, as You are mine.

Father, I pray for their restoration. The Holy Spirit teaches me what I should say. Father, I thank You for Your loving kindness and your tender mercies. You are the reason for living and breathing each day! You are the God who wipes all tears away!

I love You and I am eternally grateful for all You are and all You do. In Jesus' Name, I pray. Amen."

# RECYCLING DAY

Oftentimes, we have a hard time letting go. No matter how many times we allow people to hurt us, in whatever capacity, we find ourselves back with that same person, or with someone else who resembles the hurt the former person caused.

It is as everyone but we ourselves can see that this person is no good for us. We make excuses for why this person should stay and not go. We always think that we are the one who has the great call to *save* the person, while we ourselves become endangered and heartbroken.

We eventually lose out on the *real thing*, the *real one*, who *God* has for us, because we're so used to dealing with counterfeits.

When God began to create again, it was the artistic mind of God that spoke what was already in Him and it began to appear. God spoke: *"Light!"* and light appeared. Then God spoke: *"Sky!" In the middle of waters; separate water from water!"* The next thing God spoke was *"Separate! Water-Beneath-Heaven, gather into one place, Land, appear!"* and there it was.

God spoke: *"Earth, green up! Grow all varieties of seed-bearing plants, every sort of fruit, bearing tree."* And there it was. God spoke: *"Lights! Come out! Shine in Heaven's sky!*

*Separate day from night. Mark seasons and days and years. Lights in Heaven's sky – give light to the Earth."* And there it was.

As God continued to speak He said: *"Swarm, Ocean, with fish and all sea life! Birds fly through the sky over Earth!"* God created the huge whales, all the swarm of life in the waters, and every kind of species of flying birds. God saw that it was good. God blessed them: *"Prosper! Reproduce! Fill Ocean! Birds reproduce on Earth!"*

Finally God spoke: *"Earth, generate life! And every sort and kind: cattle and reptiles and wild animals – all kinds."* And there it was: wild animals of every kind. Cattle of all kinds, every sort of reptile and bug. God saw that it was good. God spoke: *"Let us make human beings in our image, make them reflect our nature so they can be responsible for the fish in the sea, the birds in the air, the cattle, and yes, Earth itself, and every animal that moves on the face of the Earth."*

God created human beings; He created them god-like. Reflecting God's nature. He created them male and female. God blessed them: *"Prosper! Reproduce! Fill the Earth! Take charge! Be responsible for fish in the sea and birds in the air, for every living thing that moves on the face of the Earth."*

*Then God said, "I've given you every sort of seed-bearing plant on Earth and every kind of fruit-bearing tree, given them to you for food.*

*"To all animals and birds, everything that moves and*

breathes, I give whatever grows out of the ground for food." God looked over everything He made and it was good, so very good!

In the first chapter God made man. He created man and in man's created state, He charged them to prosper, reproduce, fill the Earth, and take charge and to be responsible. However, it wasn't until the second chapter, that man was able to do what it was God created them to do. It wasn't until they began to live: "And the Lord God formed man of the dust of the ground, and breathed into his nostrils the breath of life; and man became a living soul."

When God created man He did not create man to do the job of the fish, fowl, insect or animal. When God created man, He created them to have dominion over all created things. God would come and talk to Adam in the cool of the day. But Adam, though he loved God, was still lonely. God said, it is not good for man to be alone.

After Adam named those things in the Garden over which he had been given dominion, God put Adam to sleep and out of Adam's rib God made Eve. Adam said, "This is now bone of my bones, and flesh of my flesh: she shall be called Woman, because she was taken out of Man. Therefore, shall a man leave his father and his mother, and shall cleave to his wife: and they shall be one flesh." And they both were naked, the man and his wife and were not ashamed.

Somehow, the enemy was able to come among them and cause temptation that would change the face of mankind forever.

The serpent, who was cleverer than any wild animal God had made, spoke to the Woman: *"Do I understand that God told you not to eat from any tree in the garden?" The woman said to the serpent, "Not at all. We can eat from the trees in the garden. It's only the tree in the middle of the garden that God said, 'don't eat from it; don't even touch it or you'll die.'"*

The serpent told the Woman, *"You won't die. God knows that the moment you eat from that tree; you'll see what's really going on. You'll be just like God, knowing everything, ranging all the way from good to evil."* When the Woman saw the tree looked like good eating and realized what she would get out of it –she'd know everything! – She took and ate the fruit and then gave some to her husband, and he too ate.

Immediately the two of them died *"see what was really going on"* – saw themselves naked! They sewed fig trees together as makeshift clothes for themselves. When they heard the sound of God strolling in the garden in the evening breeze, the Man and his Wife hid in the trees of the garden – they hid from God. God called to the Man: *"Where are you?"*

God asked Adam where Adam was because God no longer recognized Adam spiritually. Adam changed. His whole countenance changed. Adam said, *"I heard you in the garden and I was afraid because I was naked. And I hid."* God said, *"Who told you, you were naked? Did you eat from the tree I told you not to eat from?"*

Adam said, *"The woman you gave me as a companion,*

*she gave me fruit from the tree. And, yes, I ate it."* God said to the Woman, *"What is this that you've done?" "The serpent seduced me,"* she said *"and I ate."*

God told the serpent: *"Because you've done this, you're cursed. Cursed beyond all cattle and wild animals. Cursed to slink on your belly and eat dirt all your life. I'm declaring war between you and the Woman, between your offspring and hers. He'll wound your head, you'll wound his heel."*

He told the Woman: *"I'll multiply your pains in child-birth; you'll give birth to your babies in pain. You'll want to please your husband, but he'll lord it over you."*

He told the Man: *"Because you listened to your wife and ate from the tree that I commanded you not to eat from, 'Do not eat from this tree,' the very ground is cursed be-cause of you. Getting food from the ground will be as painful as having babies is for your wife.*

*You'll be working in pain all your life long. The ground will sprout thorns and weeds. You'll get your food the hard way, planting and tilling and harvesting. Sweating in the fields from dawn to dusk, until you return to that ground yourself, dead and buried. You started out as dirt, you'll end up dirt."*

Since then man's relationship toward each other has been changed. Adam, instead of being with Eve and do-ing what he had been created to do, was doing other things. Had Adam been with Eve instead of hanging out with his *dogs*, the enemy wouldn't have been able to breakup his happy home.

We have suffered the *repercussions* of the fall since the fall. Hearts have been broken time after time. Sometimes we suffer through relationships unnecessarily because we refuse to listen when warnings are given.

There is the still small voice on the inside of us that warns us, *this* is not the one. If we would only listen and take heed. The very thing Adam loved and longed for so much was also the very thing who caused him to fall. In his attempt to love her she introduced him to that which was forbidden. But sometimes temptation gets the best of us and we fall.

We have to be careful of those relationships with people who want to introduce us to the forbidden things, to those things we *know* we shouldn't do.

Samson and Delilah, Ahab and Jezebel, David and Bathsheba, and the list goes on. Delilah seduced Samson into revealing his strengths and weaknesses. Jezebel got close King Ahab to rule the kingdom through him, turn the people of God from God and eventually start a manhunt against God's anointed – His prophets.

David lusted after Bathsheba, causing his soldiers, her husband Uriah to die, because David's lust caused him to lie with her. Because of this, we cannot let things and people linger around us too long that shouldn't be. If we do, there is a possibility that they will take up residence where there is no room.

That's like a hoarder, continually piling up inessential, unimportant, useless things. Taking up space in every corner of our lives, until there is no way around it or out from under it. Then we eventually die from a disorder because we were trapped and didn't know how to get out.

However, the good news is, there is a way out. Adam landed us in the dilemma we're in – first sin, then death, and no one is exempt from either sin or death. We know that sin disrupted our relationship with God in every-thing and everyone. But the extent of the disturbance was not clear until God spelled it out in detail to Moses.

Death, this huge abyss separating us from God, domi-nated the landscape from Adam to Moses. Even those who didn't sin precisely as Adam did, by disobeying a specific command of God, still had to experience this termination of life, this separation from God. But Adam, who got us into this, also points ahead to the One who will get us out of it.

Here it is in a nutshell: Just as one person did it wrong and got us in all this trouble with sin and death, an-other did it right and got us out of it. But more than just getting us out of trouble, He got us into eternal life! One man said 'no' to God and put many people in the wrong. One man said 'yes' to God and put many in the right.

You don't have to settle for the counterfeit, just be pa-tient and wait on the real thing. Sometimes the one we *think* is the right one for us, ends up helping us to de-struction. Am I blaming Eve for Adam's choices? No. Do I blame the serpent? Yes. I blame the serpent because when you are in a love-filled relationship, regardless of what happens, most of the time relationships can be reconciled.

It's when we allow outside influences come in and give *unsolicited* advice, that we cause our relationship to falter and our lives to be altered. We have the ability to speak as God did: *'Stay!' 'Go!' 'Separate!*

A lot of us made the choices we made because, like in chapter one, we were created, but had not yet come alive! But now you can come, make the choice to prosper, reproduce, fill the Earth, take charge and be responsible. *You*, can tell the devil, *'No!'*

The next time you see a recycled situation or relationship, wait for garbage day and toss it in the trash. Better yet, wait for recycling day and make sure to place it in the right bin. You knew you threw it away as a newspaper, but you're wise enough to know it may show up again as a magazine! Either way, when you're done with it, off to the bin it goes!

---

## The Word:

- Genesis 1, Genesis 2:7
- Judges 16
- 2 Samuel 11
- 1 Corinthians 15:33, 1 Corinthians 6:18
- Proverbs 4:23
- 2 Corinthians 6:14
- Philippians 2:3

- Ephesians 4:31
- Numbers 16:26
- Psalm 147:3
- Psalm 73:26
- Proverbs 3:5-6
- Psalm 34:18
- Revelation 21:4
- John 14:27
- Isaiah 41:10
- Deuteronomy 31:6

## The Prayer:

"Father, You are the one who is able to keep me from falling, and to present me faultless before the presence of Your glory, with exceeding joy. You are the only wise God our Savior, to You be all the glory and majesty, dominion and power, both now and ever.

Father, help me to see when the same situation arises. Teach me to know when I'm being tempted and tried on every hand, so that I do not repeat the same trials over and over again. As I mature in You. In Jesus' Name. Amen."

# HUMBLE SOUP

*"Where did I put my small cooking pot?"* she asks to no one in particular. *"How am I going to cook this man his supper if I can never find my pots?"*

*"I must have left it at the church last Sunday at pastor's anniversary dinner. Lord Jesus, now I got to remind myself Sunday to ask the kitchen committee if they saw it. Most likely somebody already took it home and claimed it as their own."*

As Justine looked through her small refrigerator, she silently began to thank God within her heart. She remembered the times when she and Levi barely had enough food to feed the children; and many nights they went to bed hungry themselves. Today, she had so much food that she could call the neighbors over – as she often did – to give away some of the groceries she accidentally purchased over and over again.

To Justine it *wasn't* an accident purchasing the same foods; to her it was God's way of reminding her to give to others, who may be in need. So, to her, it was just in case somebody came over hungry or needed an ingredient or two, she would have enough to be the lender. God knows she remembers her days as the borrower.

*"Let me see, what can I make for dinner tonight?"* She pondered. While looking through her cabinets, she started to hum her favorite song that the choir sang

that morning, a song which she so happened to lead. *"Anyway You Fix It Lord,"* was the title of the song. She was humming the song so loud until she began to sing the song out loud, word for word. She sang in her high soprano voice. She was so engulfed in her praises to God, that she didn't hear Levi walk into the kitchen.

*"What's with all this singing, Justine? I thought God had rewound the time and we were sitting in church again,"* he said smiling from ear to ear. He enjoyed hearing his wife sing, but the game was on. Even though they had a television with surround-sound, nothing could compare to his wife's effortless range and high pitched voice.

*"I'm sorry Levi,"* she said unapologetically. *"I was looking through these cabinets, looking for my small pot, trying to find something to cook for supper tonight. Are you hungry?"*

*"I'm always hungry." Levi said playfully. "I'm going back in the living room to finish watching the game. Call me when dinner's ready."*

*"I will,"* she replied.

From the day she first laid eyes on Levi in South Carolina, Justine knew she loved him. Though he was a few years older than her, she knew from that day, he was going to marry her and make her Mrs. Wilson. *Love is* what kept them together all these years. *Love* is what caused her to bear eight babies too, she laughed to herself. But as much as she *loved* her husband, sometimes, he just got on her nerves.

Looking through her cabinets, she finally found the pot she was looking for – no, not the one she left at the church, but the pot her mother gave her when she and Levi first married. She found her *big pot.* She looked at the pot that she hadn't used in years. It was the pot that she made her *humble soup* with.

It was the soup that always reminded her that in order for her to keep the *peace* with Levi, that no matter what happens – she had to remain a dutiful and humble wife.

Now that she found the *big pot*, she thought she'd make her famous humble soup. She was certain that she had all the ingredients there in the kitchen. She went around the kitchen looking from cabinet to pantry to refrigerator, pulling out everything she'd need to make the soup delicious and fulfilling. She remembered *the joy* it brought to her family every time they sat down at the table to eat it – if only they were here to enjoy it with her and Levi today, she thought.

Justine started making her humble soup while reflecting on the pastor's sermon from earlier in the day. She thanked God for His word on *"Humility."* Her pastor, Reverend Lee Andrews, asked a few questions during the message that made her think long and hard. As a matter of fact, the questions bothered her. Though she felt upset by the questions he asked, the Spirit of the Lord chastised her quickly. Instead of her becoming conflicted, she was convicted.

He asked the church, *"What would you do with a repeat offender? Would you forgive them? Would you love them unconditionally? Or would you reject them and discard of them like yesterday's trash?"* – She sat in the choir stand and her mind wandered on to her precious children. Some of her children had done what she deemed unforgiveable toward her. Even Levi, her husband, had said some unmentionable things to her, things she never told anyone, things she dared not repeat.

But as a loving wife and mother, she was determined not to let the devil steal her *joy* or her family. She learned what it was to put her pride aside and learned to welcome *longsuffering.* She patiently endured hardships like a soldier and God knows she'd had her fair share of offenses.

With a smile on her face, she was glad that she didn't let the questions condemn her – but that she allowed the Holy Spirit to convict her into self-evaluation.

The pastor went on to say, *"If we'd be honest with ourselves, most of us, if not all of us, would eventually give up on the person and throw them away like yesterday's trash.*

*"But I'm so glad that when I was a repeat offender in the eyesight of the Lord, He still forgave me. He still loved me unconditionally. He could've rejected me – but instead, He recycled me from the trash that I was to the treasure I am. – He took the trash of yesterday, recycled me and made me meet for the Master's use today! Amen somebody?"*

Tears rolled down Justine's face as she reminisced on the *goodness* of the Lord. How *faithful* He was to her throughout the years. How she hadn't always been the best wife, mother or saint; that she too had been a repeat offender in her lifetime. But grace, mercy and the love of Christ, through the blood of Jesus, carried and sustained her.

Justine knew, without a shadow of a doubt, that the blood of Jesus saved her life. Now she looked back and wondered, how she made it over. Just as she was preparing to cut the carrots for the soup, her doorbell rang. *"Who could it be this time of day? It's almost five in the afternoon."* When she opened the door, she stifled her excitement. She couldn't believe her eyes!

*"Hey babies! You all must've smelled that pot boiling!"* One by one she kissed them on their cheek as they made their way into the kitchen. Carol, Louise and Barbara walked just like Justine, tall, upright with just enough switch and just enough strut.

*"Hey mama, what you cooking?"* Barbara asked. *"I'm hungry."*

*"Yeah, you're always hungry!"* Louise joked. *"Yeah, and you're always in my business,"* Barbara retorted. *"Listen you two, don't be in here carrying on, you ain't too grown to get ya behinds whooped,"* Justine said while handing Barbara the knife and carrots, Louise the chicken to clean and Carol the spices to put into the pot.

*"I'm glad ya'll are here. Now ya'll can finish up the soup, I'm tired."* Justine said as she took a seat at the kitchen table.

*"Carol, you're awfully quiet today,"* Justine said.

*"Yeah that's a first."* Louise joked while nudging Barbara who held in her laugh. Justine held up her big wooden spoon, giving them a warning.

*"I'm okay, ma? How much pepper am I supposed to put in this soup?"* Carol asked.

*"Here let me show you,"* Justine said, getting up. *"Has anybody seen your oldest sister?"*

*"Yeah, I spoke to Bell yesterday. She was trying to make it up here today, but you know she couldn't find anybody to keep them kids,"* Carol replied.

*"I miss my baby, I don't get a chance to see her that much. But, I keep her, Artie and those children in my prayers."* Justine said; adding pepper to the soup. *"Were you paying attention?"* she asked Carol.

Just then the door opened, and in walked Ernie, Willie and Andrew. Before they could close the door, Junior – her eldest son – walked in with flowers behind his back. He held up his finger to his lips to shush them.

*"You know I'm glad to see my babies,"* Justine said.

*"We're glad to see you too, mama,"* they replied – almost in unison. *"And so are we,"* Junior said.

At that moment Justine turned around and grabbed her chest, to make sure her heart was still beating.

She ran and gave each of her boys a big hug. She cried and took the roses Junior had for her. She couldn't believe it. *God,* she thought, *"thank you!"*

*"Levi, Levi!"* Justine yelled from the kitchen toward the living room. *"Levi, come quick!"*

*"What's with all this damn ruckus going on out here? You're going to be the death of me yet, woman."* Levi said emerging from the living room.

*"Well, I'll be..."*

Levi stood still for a few moments. Surprised to see his children standing there, side by side with their mother, his wife, he looked at them and said, *"What the hell are you waiting for? Somebody come over here and show the old man some love!"*

*"Hey pops,"* they all replied with hugs and handshakes.

Time passed by. Levi was watching the game with the boys while the girls washed, dried and put away the dishes. Justine sat at the table feeling a sense of gratitude. Today was a day that definitely caused her to feel a bit *meeker.* Comparing her situation to those of her friends, Justine felt like the most blessed woman on earth.

She had been blessed with eight wonderful offspring and too many grandchildren to name. Her blessings didn't make her feel better than anyone else – they just reminded her, she was loved.

The doorbell rang, interrupting her thoughts. *"Can somebody get the door please?"* Carol asked, putting the last dish back in the china cabinet where it belonged.

*"Who is it?"* Louise asked.

*"Delivery,"* the voice on the other side of the door replied.

*"Delivery? On a Sunday? I didn't order anything,"* Justine said.

When Louise opened the door, there stood their oldest sister Bell and her husband Artie. *"Sorry, we're late, mama. Happy Birthday!"* Justine had totally forgotten it was her birthday.

With tears in her eyes, Justine hugged her eldest daughter and son-in-law. She believed that the Lord wouldn't allow this day to pass without *all* her children being there together. She always had *faith* in God. She believed whenever she prayed and carried her family in her heart, that He'd soon answer. Lo and behold, He surely outdid Himself.

Carol pulled out the cake plates as the men emerged from the living room, some looking defeated while others smiled mischievously. She saw the look on Levi's face and laughed to herself. She knew that look, it told her what he'd never admit – his team lost and one of those boys beat him out of all his money.

She thought to herself, I bet it was Willie. Willie has a *gentleness* about him. But she also knew better, there was nothing weak about Willie. However well-mannered he was, she knew that he had a little gambling problem. She'd just pray. And Levi, though he's a tough one, has shown much *temperance* in his later years. I guess that's where Junior, Ernie and Andrew get it from.

After finishing their cake and saying their goodbyes, Justine decided to call it a night. After looking over the kitchen one last time, she made sure all the doors were locked and the windows shut tight before going into the living room to check on Levi.

Upon entering the living room, she saw that Levi had fallen asleep in his recliner. Instead of waking him up, she went to the closet, got a blanket, covered him with it, kissed him on his forehead and went to her bedroom.

Justine pulled back the covers and prepared for bed. But first she knelt down to pray. When she lay down she reached for her bible and began to read Galatians 5:22-23: *"But the fruit of the Spirit is love, joy, peace, longsuffering, gentleness, goodness, faith, meekness, temperance, against such there is no law. And they that are Christ's"*

Justine fell asleep while reading her bible. She had a dream that night. She dreamt that she was standing in her kitchen dressed in an all-white gown. Oddly, she had no shoes on. While surveying the familiar kitchen, she noticed on her table a sign that had the letters RSVP written it gold. On it, her name; JUSTINE WILSON, written below in red lettering.

Unconsciously she began to move toward the table, noticing that the chair had already been pulled out. As she sat down at the table she noticed a bowl and a spoon. Looking at the bowl, she could smell the sweet aroma that came from it. She knew exactly what it was, her *humble* soup.

She looked inside the bowl and saw the ingredients which she used. She also saw alphabets floating around in the bowl of soup. The strange thing is she never made alphabet soup. She took her spoon and began to stir it – the more she stirred the more the letters formed and before she knew it, she was able to read what the soup had written:

*"When He finally arrives, blazing in beauty and all
His angels with Him, the Son of Man will take
His place on His glorious throne.
Then all the nations will be arranged before Him and
will sort the people out, much as a Shepherd sorts out
sheep and goats, putting sheep to His right
and goats to His left.*

*Then the King will say to those on His right,
'Enter, you who are blessed by my Father!
Take what's coming to you in this kingdom.
It's been ready for you since the world's foundation.
And here's why.*

*'I was hungry and you fed me,
I was thirsty and you gave me a drink,
I was homeless and you gave me a room,*

*I was shivering and you gave me clothes,*
*I was sick and you stopped to visit,*
*I was in prison and you came to me.'*

*Then those 'sheep' are going to say,*
*'Master, what are you talking about?*
*When did we ever see you hungry and not feed you?*
*And when did we ever see you sick*
*or in prison and come to you?'*
*Then the King will say, 'I'm telling the solemn truth:*
*Whenever you did one of these things*
*to someone overlooked or ignored,*
*that was me – you did it to me."*

That night, Justine heard the *King* speak to her. Every time she took in a stranger. Every time she fed a neighbor. Every time she gave someone a piece of clothing. Every time she visited someone in prison, whether with her church or a loved one. Every time she went to a shelter and fed the hungry or ministered to someone at a bus stop or in the hospital.

Every time she fed someone her humble soup, she was portraying the love of God. All she did – she did it unto the Lord.

While Levi slept soundly, Justine slipped away to be with the Lord. With her bible in hand, and glasses on her face, she slept peacefully. Her body lay without a care as her soul walked up the stairs that led her to heaven's gates. Once she reached the gates, she stood in the judgment as her name had been written in the

*Lamb's Book of Life.* There it was, written in the *blood of the Lamb.*

Without a care in the world and a clue as to what she left behind her, she began to rejoice as she heard the words she was *dying* to hear her whole *life,*

"Well done, good and faithful servant; thou hast been faithful over a few things, I will make you ruler over many things: enter thou into the joy of the Lord."

| The Word: |
|---|

- Deuteronomy 15:7
- 2 Chronicles 7:14
- Psalm 37:21
- Proverbs 22:6
- Matthew 25:23, 31-40
- John 21:1-14
- Philippians 2:3-11
- James 4:6
- Matthew 18:1-4
- 1 Peter 5:5-6
- 2 Chronicles 34:27
- 1 Peter 3:3-4
- Colossians 3:12
- James 3:13
- Matthew 6:2

## The Prayer:

"Father, it's in the Name of Jesus that I come to You today. Thank You for your Spirit, thank You for forgiving my sins. Thank You for Your love. Without You, I am nothing. Thank You for humbling Yourself to the Cross, so that I could humble myself to salvation. In Jesus' Name. Amen."

# BEHOLD, THE BRIDEGROOMS' COMING

Something old, something new, something borrowed, something blue. I hope that what they say is true.

*"Lord, I hope this thing works out, this is my last chance to be married and I don't want to blow this one!"* said Lila.

*"What was that you said, honey?"* Her mother asked.

*"Oh nothing, mother dear, just thinking out loud,"* she responded. Lila made a mental note to herself to be careful what she said. She couldn't afford to be heard saying such things. If people knew that her heart wasn't really convinced she should be marrying Jacob, she'd be ruined. She must walk down that aisle, smile her prettiest smile, and show her pearly whites. She'd invested enough in the porcelain veneers and now they'd really pay off.

They are what attracted Jacob to her in the first place. She noticed him looking across the restaurant at her for some time. She looked at him and thought to herself *'how pathetic.'* She had a really bad habit of thinking out loud. Sometimes she thought something and spoke it without even realizing that she was doing so.

Her friend Tammy asked her what was so pathetic and

she responded by using her eyes to point in Jacob's direction. Tammy casually turned her head as if she were looking for the waitress, who served their table, when she noticed the guy Lila was referring to sitting at a table across from them, alone.

*"That's not pathetic, Lila. That's just a man who knows how to enjoy his own company. Sometimes I take myself on a date. I'm learning to love myself so when Mr. Right comes along, I can say to Mr. Right 'Now, so long!' You know what I mean, girl?"* said Tammy with a chuckle.

*"No, I don't know what you mean. I mean I'm fabulous all around and though I don't need a man to complete me, it'll sure be nice to have someone in the middle of the night when I'm all alone, and all my batteries are gone."* Lila laughed.

*Lila!* Said Tammy. *The devil is a liar! Girl, you better wait on Jesus!*

*"Yeah, Tammy, I've been waiting on Jesus for a long time. Just to let you know if you didn't already know, Jesus ain't marrying nobody, neither is he making love to anyone. I need somebody who is rough, rugged and righteously ridiculous in the bedroom. Oh, he also has to have a career, a 401k, love the Lord, and attend church, and bible study at least twice a month.*

*"He can't be a preacher, deacon or any of the type. I can't be in church fighting over no man. He must love his mother, and I definitely don't want to marry a Tarzan just to find out when the lights go out, he likes to play Jane.*

They looked at each other, gave one another a high five and said, *"Okaaaaay!"*

*"You remember that last spectacle I went through at Mt. Pisgah? I thought I had me a strong brother, but he liked my brother,"* said Lila bitterly.

*"Yeah, I remember that girl. That was messed up. By the way, how is your little brother, Darrin doing?"* Tammy asked.

*"My brother is fine – I guess. I wish him all the best. Hope him and what's his name from Mt. Pisgah is living it up. My mother said I should forgive Darrin and move on. Darrin didn't know that Mr. Mt. Pisgah and I were dating in the first place.*

*"You know, I was so in love with that man. And he was packing something serious. You know you don't always get a fine brother with a nice piece. I wonder who the top is and who the bottom is in that relationship. Nope! Nope! I don't want to know! Lord Jesus, I just had a vision.*

*"Tammy are you listening to me?"*

*"Yeah girl I was listening, but I kind of tuned you out after you started talking about Daemon or as you call him, Mr. Mt. Pisgah. Girl, no offense, but I am tired of hearing you talk about that like it happened yesterday. It's been two and a half years and you're still bitter about it.*

*"Your brother Darrin's been gay since gay was gay.*

*Daemon had no idea Darrin was your brother until he showed up with him at your mother's house for Christmas that year. If you weren't so secretive and had introduced him to your mother, you wouldn't have found out the way you did.*

*"But, on the other hand, God has a way of revealing things. And honey, that was a Christmas present I'm sure you weren't expecting and one you'll never forget,"* said Tammy.

*"Whose side are you on?"* Lila questioned.

*"I'm on the Lord's side."* Tammy replied.

*"And so am I,"* said the unfamiliar male voice.

*"And who are you?"* Lila asked.

*"I'm Jacob. I couldn't help but notice you sitting here from across the room. I saw that you two were in an intense conversation. I didn't want to be rude, so I waited for an opportunity to come over and introduce myself. And you are?"* He asked extending his hand toward Lila.

*"I am about to leave. Come on Tammy. Let's pay the bill and go,"* said Lila.

*"The bill has already been taken care of. I paid it when I first noticed you sitting here. I said to myself 'a fine girl like that should never have to pay for anything else ever again, in her life. I took one look at you and knew how Adam felt when he first saw Eve, Wo-man!*

*"So once again, I'd like to introduce myself, I'm Jacob. And you are?"*

*"She's Lila. Her name is Lila Brighton, right Lila,"* said Tammy, nudging Lila.

*"Yes – uh – yes, my name is Lila and I need to be excused."* With that Lila got up and went to the ladies' room. Soon Tammy followed.

*"Girl, what is wrong with you? You got Mr. Work-it-out sitting right in front of you and you go running to the bathroom. The devil is a liar! Now move out of the mirror so I can reapply my lipstick. Honey, if you don't want Mr. I-Don't-Wanna-Do-Wrong, then I'm gonna sop him up like mama's biscuits,"* said Tammy.

*"What happened to all that talk about saving yourself for Jesus?"* Lila asked.

*"Girl, you didn't hear your sermon at the table tonight? You said, 'Jesus ain't marrying anybody, neither is he making love to anyone,' and..."*

"Yeah, I know what I said, Tammy."

*"Here,"* Tammy said, handing Lila a dollar.

*"Girl, what's this?"*

*"That's your offering. I want to thank you for that word, and I wanted to sow a seed in your life, because I believe that Jacob's about to sow a seed in mine!,"* said Tammy, walking out the bathroom.

Five minutes later Lila came out of the bathroom to find Tammy sitting there with mascara smudged on the corners of her eyes. *'Here Delilah!'*

*"What's with the attitude and what's with this dollar bill ministry? My words of inspiration?"* Lila asked sarcastically.

*"No, Mr. I-Don't-Wanna-Do-Wrong left me his number to give to you. I told him you weren't interested. But he looked at me and said, 'she may not be interested, but God is!'"*

That was a year and seven months ago. Lila looked down at the card that he'd left for her and there it read, *Jacob D. Tilley, Esq.* For one week she looked at that card, and every time she looked at it she saw dollar signs. Lila wondered if *Mr. Esq.* had dollars or cents. She'd soon find out.

Lila and her girlfriends started hanging tough. She began clubbing again; and the more she partied, the less she attended church. She stopped hanging out with Tammy all together. Tammy started dating some local up-and-coming preacher. To Lila, he was a *no-body.* She was like, *Chile-boo!* If he ain't *mega,* then I won't be *minor.* Tammy talked with Lila on occasion and she kept telling Lila she was praying for her and that she needed to get back to church. *No thanks and ma'am!*

Lila's good, good girlfriends Chanel, Gucci, Prada and Yves, were always with her; that is, she was always with them. They stripped at the club where Lila hosted. She knew all those ministerial classes she had taken *"would* someday *work out for my good."*

Lila knew how to *woo* the crowd, amp the people up and get that money coming in, just like she saw her former pastor do. *He had them women mortgaging their homes off so that he could live lavishly. All with the promise of marriage – gullible fools.*

In the club is where Lila would run into Jacob again. *What is he doing at the club?* She looked at him and said *so much for his godly convictions.* When he noticed Lila, she made a bee line toward the bathroom but couldn't get to it because of all the patrons waiting on line. *Damn!* she thought.

*"I enjoyed you up there tonight,"* said Jacob.

Lila turned around, showing all of her porcelain veneers and said, 'Oh, hey, Joseph, no, that's Jimmy. No, that's not it either, Justin, ump, Jared, is it? Lila was pretending not to remember his name.

*"It's Jacob,"* he said.

*"Oh yeah. Jacob, how are you? What are you doing here?"* Lila asked.

*"I'm here tonight, looking to wrestle with an angel. Nah, I'm really here trying to find my sister Gina. She goes by the stage name Gucci. My mother has been pressing me to come in here and drag Gina out of here, if need be.*

*"They told me she's backstage changing. I'm waiting for her, until then I've been handing out cards,"* Jacob said over the loud music and roaring crowd.

"Cards?"

"Yes, my mom is the pastor at Kingdom Building Victorious Church, it's a mile from here. We believe in Rescuing, Rebuilding, and Restoring and Renewing people in the Kingdom of God. How about you? What are you really doing in here, Lila--or should I say Delilah?" He asked.

"As you can see, I am the hostess with the mo-stess. Corny, I know," said Lila with a laugh. Gina, better known as Gucci, made her way toward them. "Hey, Jacob, I'm getting off in a few, what are you doing when you leave here?" Lila asked.

"Well I'm dropping her off at the church," Jacob said pointing to Gina, his sister. "We're having all -night prayer. Mama's been preaching about the Second Coming of the Lord these last few weeks. So we've been in what the church calls a shut-in. You want to join us?" he asked.

"For prayer and shut-in? Oh no! But I just may come by the church on Sunday. I'll see. Will you be there?" Lila asked.

"I'm always there. I have to be. I'm the assistant pastor now. My father died a year ago. You know God always has a way for you to answer your call – even if it is through the loss of a loved one. But hey, all is fair in love. If you don't believe me, you should ask Stevie Wonder. Remember, Lila, love is blind," he said smiling.

They said their goodbyes and that Sunday she was at the church right in time to hear the message coming from Overseer Victoria Tilley. She was a tall, beautiful woman. She looked no more than forty but was well over sixty. She preached about being ready when the Lord came back. That day Lila went to the altar, and gave her hand to the preacher, but she didn't give her heart to God; and today she knew that she wouldn't be giving it to Jacob either.

*"Come on girl, you're already an hour late,"* Lila's mother warned.

*"They can wait, it's my day!"* Lila screamed, trying to use her hands to remove the wrinkles from her dress. She decided she'd better let the wrinkles be. Her dress was becoming more and more stained as she touched it. A few moments ago she heard what sounded like thunder and cursed the rain.

*"Hell, where is Gina?"* she thought. Gucci was her Maid of Honor, and right now she needed a maid before she went off on somebody and lost her honor.

Bad enough she had to act like she was so in love with God. What she was in love with was Jacob's portion of the multimillion dollar life insurance policy left from his father and the firm his father left him. Money made her say, *hallelujah* all day!

*Gina!* She called and there was no answer. *Gucci!* She called again and still, no answer. *Where could she possibly have gone? It's my wedding and I have to do everything!* Lila said angrily. *Gina are you in here?* No answer. *Mother! Have you seen Gina? ...Mother?* Still, no response. Lila looked to the far corner of the room and saw the dress her mother had worn, lying on the floor along with her glasses and jewelry.

Frantically she searched the room and all she could do to keep her composure was to convince herself, this must be a prank. That was until she heard a scream. When she ran to the room reserved for the bridal party she saw Yves, Prada, Chanel and Gucci standing side by side looking down at the dress Overseer Victoria Tilley, Jacob's mother, had worn, along with her bible.

*"We were standing here talking to mother. She was reading a passage of scripture and all of a sudden, we heard thunder, and she was gone. She disappeared just like that. I, we heard you calling but we, I couldn't respond. What's going on? – Jacob, we must get to the church,"* Gucci said.

When they pulled up to the church there was no rain. It hadn't rained at all, not a cloud in the sky. *Then what was all that thunder about,* they all thought silently. There was a small crowd gathered outside of the church with people pacing and screaming. Lila jumped out of the car, past the crowd and wondering eyes.

She ran into the church, and down the aisle. The more she ran, the dirtier her dress became. The more she ran, the filthier she became. She ran around the sanctuary screaming Jacob's name. All she could see was a heap of clothing – the tuxedo he had worn while waiting at the altar for her arrival.

She grabbed the tuxedo and sobbed. She realized that she really did love him and the love she lost was now gone forever. It was too late. She looked around the church and she saw that there were many pieces of clothing that lay in the pews where the guests had sat.

Lila then remembered last week's message. Overseer Tilley stood tall and powerful. Yet she had a faint sadness that crept across her face. She prayed that morning as the church stood still. It was so quiet. It was a dreary feeling. That morning she wept. She wept as if she was in mourning. Lila didn't understand what Overseer Tilley was mumbling about.

Her mumbling turned into sobs and finally her sobs turned into a bitter cry. *"The Lord is soon to come! Get right with God, the Lord is soon to come!"* said Overseer Tilley.

Lila sat frozen and heart hardened as others flooded the altar. That morning, Overseer Tilley prayed and many received Salvation. But, for some reason Lila refused to move. Lila had heard this same message all of her life and chalked it up to be a fairy tale. The Second Coming of the Lord Jesus Christ was no more real to her then reading the story about the Wiz.

Everyone believed in the Wiz, but never saw him – until the end. Even then what they needed to prepare themselves to get back to Kansas, they awoke to find out they had been there all along.

Like Dorothy, Lila didn't have enough vision to move

*pass her past* and move *forward* in God. Like the Scarecrow, Lila felt like *garbage – a fool – brainless.* Lila was so wicked that she didn't let her *thoughts* go toward the Lord. Like the Tin Man, she was *heartless, full of pride* and lacked *true love.* Finally, like the Lion, Lila was *beautiful* and *fearless* on the outside but had no *faith* on the inside – no *courage*; she had lost her faith, embittered by her past.

Lila looked back on that day. She could hear Overseer Tilley preaching, "*Ready or Not, Here He Comes,*" and reading:

*"God's Kingdom is like ten virgins who took oil lamps and went out to greet the bridegroom. Five were silly and five were smart. The silly virgins took lamps, but no extra oil. The smart virgins took jars of oil to feed their lamps. The bridegroom didn't show up when they expected, and they fell asleep.*

*"In the middle of the night someone yelled out, 'He's here! The Bridegroom's here! Go out and greet Him!'"*

*"The ten virgins got their lamps ready. The silly virgins said to the smart ones, 'Our lamps are going out; lend us some of your oil.' They answered, 'There might not be enough to go around; go buy your own.'*

*"They did, but while they were out buying oil, the Bridegroom arrived. When everyone who was there to greet him had gone into the wedding feast, the door was locked. Much later, the other virgins, the silly ones,*

*showed up and knocked on the door, saying, 'Master, we're here. Let us in.' He answered, 'Do I know you? I don't think I know you.'*

*"So stay alert. You have no idea when He might arrive."*

"It's too late," Lila grieved. "The Bridegroom has come and gone. Here we sit like fools. Yves, Chanel, Prada and even Gucci—we are all left behind. We didn't heed the warning. We didn't prepare our lamps with oil.

We sat in church Sunday after Sunday and still, not prepared. All I have to show for it is a dirty bridal gown with no wedding to attend. No husband to exchange vows with and no wedding feast to celebrate. I waited too long. I missed my way back to heaven – I missed the *Bridegroom!*"

*Ready or Not, Here He Comes!* Will *you* be ready?

| The Word: |
|:---:|

- Proverbs 11:1-3
- Proverbs 8:22
- Proverbs 27:6
- Proverbs 30:32
- Matthew 6:19-21
- Matthew 24:32-44
- Matthew 25:1-13
- Luke 12:15
- 1 Thessalonians 5:2-4

- 2 Thessalonians 3:10
- 2 Peter 3:10
- Hebrews 3:8-18
- Revelation 16:15
- Matthew 24:4-5; 11; 23-27

## The Prayer:

"Father in the Name of Jesus, I come to You repenting of my sins. I first ask You to come into my heart and to cleanse me from all unrighteousness. Father, I ask that You would help me with the iniquity and the hardness that's in my heart, which has been holding me back and keeping me from progressing forward.

I pray, Father, that You would forgive me of every trespass, as I forgive those who have trespassed against me. Today, I want a heart that forgives. I let go of all disappointments and the disastrous choices I made. I pray now, that You would remove this heart of stone and give me a heart of flesh.

I lay it all at the altar – the place of exchange. I want to be ready when the Bridegroom comes. In Jesus' Name, I pray. Amen."

# ALL ABOARD

"*Gerald, are you taking the train home today after work or are you driving?*" Gerald's co-worker Alicia asked.

"*I believe I'll be taking the train home tonight, Alicia. I didn't drive in today and my wife is working late, so she won't be able to pick me up. Why'd you ask?*"

"*Well, Marlon is home sick. He can't pick me up tonight, so I have to take the train and I didn't want to get on the train by myself. I hate taking public transportation, especially during rush hour.*"

"*It seems like it should be called indolent hour, because those trains are painfully slow during the evening commute,*" Alicia said.

"*Well, don't worry. Just let me know when you're clocking out and I'll leave along with you,*" Gerald said. "*We can both take the northbound number four train to the Bronx. You'll get off at 125th Street and I'll keep going to 161st St. Deal?*"

"*Deal,*" she replied.

"*Hey Stacey girl, are you still going to the club with me tonight?*" Marla asked her friend while clocking out from work.

"No, Marla, I promised my mom, I'd go with her to church tonight."

"Church! Girl, come over here, lean closer."

"For what? Marla, what are you doing?" Stacey asked.

"I'm checking your forehead to see if you have a fever or something. Are you feeling okay? Talking about you going to somebody's church," Marla asked her.

"Yeah girl, I'm feeling great. I'm actually looking forward to going. They said there is this guest preacher coming in from out of town and I need a word from the Lord. It's been a while since I even thought about going to church. You know, after I had Tiffany, the church wasn't so nice to me.

"I remember when they had me stand up in front of the congregation and apologize for getting pregnant. I was so embarrassed and ashamed. It took me a long time to forgive my mother for that. I expected her to take up for me. I thought she was more interested in what the church people had to say, and how they felt, rather than in defending me.

"Now that I look back at it, I respect my mother's decision. It wasn't about the church or what they had to say, but it was about the word of God and what He has to say. Daughter or not, the word of God doesn't change," Stacey said.

"Well, you go on and praise the Lord, girl. I'm going to the club tonight to see the strippers and have my own little revival. Are you taking the train tonight?"

114

*"Yes, the number four train. I'll wait for you and we can take the train together,"* Stacey replied.

*"Okay, I'm going to run to the bathroom. Here, hold my pocketbook. I'll be out in a few minutes, then we can go."*

*"You got it,"* Stacey said.

*"What do you mean; you can't see me tonight because your wife didn't go away?"* Charles yelled impatiently into his cell phone receiver. *"We've been planning this for weeks. I've been looking forward to spending some time with you. Look, Jamal, if we aren't going to spend more time together, then we need to just break up! I'm so sick and tired of playing second fiddle to your wife. I can have any man I want, and you know it. But it's you that I love. I love you!*

*"Excuse me, what did you say?"* Charles asked Jamal as as he spoke loudly, causing concerned stares of those who passed by.

*"Yeah, I knew you were married when I met you; and yeah, I knew you had children. But remember this, Mr. Man, you pursued me, deacon. I did not pursue you."* With that, Charles hit the end call button on his cell phone and made his way to the northbound number four train.

Jamal looked at his phone in disbelief. He couldn't believe that Charles was yelling at him and then had the nerve to hang up on him. Yes, he and his wife were having trouble in their marriage, and were even talking divorce. But they were trying to work it out for the sake of their children and, because deep down inside, they really loved and cared for each other.

Allison, Jamal's wife, loved him unconditionally. She loved him past his cheating ways and proclivities to sin. As a matter of fact, she knew all about Jamal and his *strange desires.* That didn't keep her from falling in love with him, and her mind from thinking that she could help him change those desires. She knew as well as he did that only *God* could help him, and all she could do was love him.

Thinking about his wife and children, Jamal smiled to himself. He hated what he had become, and he hated having met Charles on Facebook, even more.

First, their conversation had been based on ministry and God. That's how Jamal found out that Charles was the minster of music over at Tabernacle of Faith. That's how Charles learned Jamal was the Chairman of the Deacon Board over at Greater Faith Cathedral.

Soon their two paths met face-to-face when the pastors and congregants of both Tabernacle of Faith and Greater Faith began to fellowship. Jamal and Charles became best of friends. However, Jamal's pastor warned him that, as a married man, it wasn't good for him to hang out with single men; because hanging out with single men meant he would open himself up to temptations.

He recommended that Jamal and his wife find company

with other married saints. Jamal's pastor hadn't suspected an intimate relationship between Jamal and Charles. Rather, his warnings were based solely on the adventures of single men compared to the commitment of those who were married.

Jamal turned off his computer at work. He, too, rushed toward the number 4 train. He and Allison were going away this weekend to a Christian couples retreat up in the mountains. His prayer was that he would remember why he fell in love with the woman he married, and the importance of denying his own desires in order to be the father and husband God had called him to be. He was certain that he could be that and more—in time.

*"This is the Woodlawn-bound number four train; the next stop is Grand Central—42ⁿᵈ Street. Stand clear of the closing doors, please..."* the voice of the computerized train conductor announced as the doors closed.

*"For God so loved the world that He gave His only begotten Son, that whosoever believeth in Him should not perish, but have everlasting life. The Lord is soon to come. Whether you're black or white, rich or poor. There is but one way to God and that's through Jesus. After death comes the judgment, people. Jesus loves you. He died for you and He is coming again."*

*"You don't have to perish; you can be saved today. The Bible says, "The wages of sin is death, but the gift of God is eternal life. Jesus said, 'I've come that they might have life and have it more abundantly.' If you confess with your mouth the Lord Jesus and believe in your heart that*

*God has raised Him from the dead, you will be saved..."*

The evangelist made her plea to the people on the north-bound number four train. She hadn't noticed the home-less man half asleep in the corner. Terry heard this lady make the same plea daily. He, too, remembered his days of going to church. He smiled and thought to himself his favorite scripture, *"I have learned, whatsoever state I am, therewith to be content."*

He remembered being faithful to Mount Hebron Cathedral and how he had loved being in church so much that he would go to all three services. Though faithful, he never really did fit in with the saints at the church. He often tried to be a part of the ministries there, but they never took him seriously.

He and his wife Melissa were there all of the time. However, everyone loved and respected Melissa because *she* gave all of the time. She and Terry both were tith-ers and they gave liberally. However, she gave because she realized that it was in her giving that the pastor and trustees recognized her. Eventually, she was placed on the trustee board of the church.

Unbeknownst to the church, it was Terry who brought home a six-figure salary, and that most of the contri-butions given were through him. But there were times when he was taken aback by some of the messages his pastor preached. This pastor always bragged about how many degrees he had, how much money he acquired and the size of his home. Every message was pretty-much about being prosperous. But there were people in Mt. Hebron Cathedral with overflowing bank accounts but whose souls were bankrupt. The devil was surely coming after them to pay up on their debts.

As Melissa's notoriety grew, she started to resent Terry. She began to compare him to the pastor and the men at church. When he found out that she had been having an affair with Deacon Frazier, it literally broke his heart. He tried to reconcile with her but she refused. She ended up divorcing him and marrying Deacon Frazier, taking more than half of what he had worked for so many years to build for the two of them.

She took the home, the cars and most of the money. He was angry but he didn't tell the judge that he was abusive and neglectful. He didn't stand a chance in that courtroom, especially when the letter of divorce was read—a letter his very own pastor signed! When Melissa divorced him, his spirit broke. Then, less than a year later, Deacon Frazier had left Melissa, realizing that she had nothing. All she had belonged to Terry. She lost her notoriety in the church and was eventually asked to step down from the board of trustees.

Terry remembered the days when he lost everything—he lost everything but his *hope*. Yes, he was a homeless man on the street with a doctorate degree. One would never know. How could he remain Dr. Terry Williamson and counsel others when he himself was broken?

The Evangelist Mary Hopkins continued with her plea of sinners to salvation.

"*Amen,*" Gerald declared while the evangelist continued.

Some praised loudly, while others like Marla became irritated. *"This lady is really killing my vibe, yo'. She gonna make me miss the club tonight with all this Jesus talk."*

While Marla complained, Stacey silently listened, as did Alicia, who paid close attention to her co-worker Gerald. She knew that he went to church, and every day he spoke to her about the Lord and how God loved her. He demonstrated his walk with God in every way. When she had her office indiscretion with another employee, everyone in the office talked about it and cast judgment on her. But Gerald never said anything except to go in her cubicle and pray.

*"I hope this lady shut up already,"* Charles said, waking up Terry, the homeless man.

*"What are you looking at?"* Charles asked Terry, rolling his eyes.

*"I'm looking at you! Remember, you're taking a ride in my car, even if you did pay $2.75 to get in it. I'd appreciate it if you'd tone down your voice. A brother trying to get his sleep on over here. If you were smart, you'd listen to what the lady was saying, instead of sitting here looking like you angry with the world!"*

Charles thought about what the homeless man had just spoken. True, Charles was angry and he was taking his anger out on both the lady and the homeless guy. He began to mope silently; and then he asked God to forgive him. He decided that night on that train he was no longer going to be with Jamal. He realized that what he felt was more of an infatuation than love, and that Jamal belonged to Allison and those three beautiful kids they shared. He didn't want to be the reason why that family was destroyed. *"God, I'm sorry. I repent,"* he began praying.

During this time, the train was moving extremely fast—faster than usual. As the evangelist held onto the handle bar above her, she continued, *"If you desire to receive the Lord Jesus, you can pray along with me. Don't be ashamed. The word of God says, 'Whoever is ashamed of me and my words, the Son of Man will be ashamed of them when He comes in His glory and in the glory of the Father and of the holy angels...' Come on, let's pray. It's simple. Just repeat after me...*

*"God, I know that I am a sinner. I know that I deserve the consequences of my sin. However, I am trusting in Jesus Christ as my Savior. I believe that His death and resurrection provided for my forgiveness. I trust in Jesus and Jesus alone as my personal Lord and Savior. Thank you, Lord, for saving me and forgiving me! Amen!"*

*"Amen!"*

Evangelist Mary Hopkins could not believe the number of resounding voices she heard coming from the people on the train. All these people praying and believing God were here. She was so excited and thankful to the Lord. She had been trying to get the evangelism team at her local church to do some evangelizing with her.

She felt that the church had lost its desire to do outreach. But she believed that if she was consistent, the Lord would bless and draw the people to Himself as He promised. All she'd have to do is lift *Him* up.

Evangelist Mary Hopkins continued throughout the car, handing out tracts and flyers with the name of her church and pastor written on the back. She believed that it was her God-given duty to evangelize; and she made sure she was a witness every day. She knew also that, with the prayers of the saints over at Mission Outreach, while she was out every day witnessing to the lost, she was covered in prayer. That the Spirit of the Lord would draw the people once the invitation was given.

Just as she handed her last tract to a young woman who had refused, there was a loud bang!

People began to scream and fall on top of each other. Everything went black and that was all she remembered.

*"Am I dreaming? What's going on?"* Marla asked out loud. She started choking because of the thickness of the smoke surrounding her. *"Oh God, where AM I? I can't see,"* she cried. *"Help, help me! Somebody, please get me out of here!"*

*"There has to be a way out,"* she reasoned. She remembered that she was on the train with Stacey. *Okay, Marla, girl. Calm yourself down and think. You just have to find Stacey and get out of here,"* she said to herself.

Just as she began to move, she cried out in pain. Her leg was broken and she couldn't get up. She started hearing cries all around her. Slowly she looked around through the darkness, trying to see a glimpse of some-one—*anyone*. She couldn't see through the thick dark-ness. But she *could feel* everything that was happening around her, and she didn't like the fear she was feeling.

*"Alicia! Alicia! Where are you? Are you okay? Are you hurt?"* Gerald asked. He was hoping that Alicia was somewhere near. They were sitting next to one another on the train. But now the seat was emptied and he was there alone. *Where did the people go?* He asked himself.

*"This must be some sick joke or something. Is anybody out there?"* He heard some movement that startled him, but still no answer from Alicia.

However, he did hear some faint cries and a few moans here and there. He couldn't believe what he saw next.

*"What is this? I can't believe what is happening! I knew I shouldn't have gotten on this train. This train...okay, what happened to the train? Where am I? I demand to know where I am! Somebody has some explaining to do! This is ridiculous! Damn it! Where am I?"* Charles asked.

*Wow...this is beautiful. Are those golden streets I see beyond those gates, are those mansions I see? Is that Jasper? This can't be, I must've died and gone to heaven,* Jamal said.

*"Lord have mercy, Gerald!"* Alicia screamed at the top

of her lungs, but there was no Gerald in sight. From as far as she could see, there was darkness and smoke. There were faint cries and moans coming out from all around her. She stood still in the darkness, unaware of what was happening around her. All she could do is think of how she could feel her way out of the wreckage. She knew something terrible must've happened on the train. Of all the days the train could have derailed—on the one day she decided to take it.

Terry lay silent in the darkness. Though he was confused, something told him there had been a horrible accident, and he lay victim among the ruins. He began to praise God. He thought, even though it was bad, it could be worse—he could've died. But he was still alive and grateful.

As Evangelist Mary Hopkins came to, she began to cry. Suddenly, the memory of the cries she heard from herself and the passengers, as well as the brute force of the train she felt as it flipped over, came running back to her mind. She knew all too well that she had not survived it. Though she saw herself—she could see, smell and feel around—something in her knew that she had died; and she knew that after death, came the judgment.

One by one, they began to arise from their place of lodging. There on the train, instantly they had been transported to a place that was unfamiliar. A place none of them have ever been, yet the place seemed so inviting and peaceful. Just that quickly they had forgotten about the train accident and they wondered in amazement, *'where could they possibly be?'*

*"You're at the judgment, you are not in heaven,"* the voice said.

There at the gate stood a very large being with wings that spanned across time and eternity. As they all stood, they noticed that they could hear the voice, but couldn't see the face of the being who spoke to them. Every time the being spoke a word, they were warm and comforting to those who heard them. Yet, deep within, a terror formed because within the hands of the being lay a book.

The front of the book read: *"The Lamb's Book of Life."* One by one, their names were called. They were judged right there.

There were others who were being judged from all over the world—those who, also, had died at the very same moment. Each stood in judgment alone, though. No one could vouch for the other; every man's deeds were written there in the book. Some thought they'd definitely get through, just to find out their name had been blotted out.

There they were—the dead, great and small—standing before the throne; and books were opened. Then another book was opened, the Book of Life. And the dead were judged by what was written in the book, according to what each had done. And if anyone's name was not found written in the Book of Life, he was thrown into the lake of fire.

Needless to say, all of them on that number four train didn't make it in; neither did they ever see each other again. They went into eternity; some saved, some sinners. You never know when the Lord will call your number. You may be sleeping, you may be sick, you may be in an accident or you just may be on a train.

| The Word: |
|---|

- Matthew 10:26-28
- Matthew 19:9
- John 3:16
- John 10:10
- John 14:6
- Romans 6:23
- Romans 10:9
- 1 Corinthians 6:9-11
- Revelation 20:12-15
- Revelation 21:10-27

| The Prayer: |
|---|

"Father, in the Name of Jesus, I come to You today repenting of every sin I've committed, both knowingly and unknowingly. Please, wash, clean and make me over. Any day now, the Son of Man can appear, I want to be ready when He comes. Lord, create in me a clean heart and renew within me the right Spirit.

Today, I forgive and I let go. I turn from my imminent perdition and into Your saving grace. Thank You for the blood of Jesus that was shed for me, that I may be saved and endure to the end. In Jesus' Name I pray. Amen."

# TWENTY-FIVE YEARS
# TO LIFE

*"Twenty-Five Years to Life."* That's what my sentence was. I'll never forget that day. The clock seemed to stand still in that courtroom. I could hear the reaction of those who sat behind me as the jury handed down their verdict. *Guilty of first-degree murder!*

I couldn't believe it. As I was led away in handcuffs and sent back to prison, my faith shattered into a million pieces. I couldn't believe that God would forsake me. I just knew I'd be going home. The whole case was circumstantial; there wasn't any premeditated murder as the prosecutor alleged. I was just someone trying to help a stranger.

It was a cold winter night in January. The snow was falling and I was on my way to the supermarket to do some last-minute shopping before the forecast blizzard arrived. I knew, due to the severity of the storm, that the town would be closed for days to come, including the mega-mart.

I pulled into the parking lot of the supermarket, and was lucky enough to find a parking spot right in front of the entrance. Someone else was pulling out and I had gotten there just in the nick of time. I put on my gloves and said a quick prayer as I exited my car. I prayed that the mart wouldn't be too packed, that I could get what I needed and be out of there as quickly as I entered. I went from aisle to aisle, placing in the shopping cart all the items that were on my list.

After filling my cart, I joined the others on the checkout line. While in line, I noticed a young lady smiling sheepishly at me. I couldn't help but notice how attractive she was. She was petite and curvy, with brown hair and hazel eyes. She was beautiful.

*"Sir, are you paying with cash or credit?"* the attendant asked.

*"Oh, I'm sorry; I'll be paying with cash,"* I replied.

Walking out of the mart with my purchases, I couldn't help but feel a little embarrassed. *How long was I staring at the young lady in the line? Did anyone notice me? Did I hold up the line?* These were some of the questions I asked myself while making my way to the car. I knew one thing: She was beautiful and she'd be a face I'd never forget. I thought to myself, if she lived in town, why hadn't I seen her before today? And, if she did God willing, I'd bump into her again.

I loaded my purchases into the trunk of my car and closed the hood. I noticed her standing there in the parking space opposite me. She looked a little disheveled standing in front of her small, compact vehicle. She sighed loudly and struggled to put her groceries in her car. I noticed, as she closed the back seat of the car door why she was sighing: there was steam rising from the hood of her car. That's when my whole life changed for the worst.

*"Excuse me, ma'am, is everything all right?"* I asked her.

*"It seems my engine done gone out on me again,"* she replied.

*"I just got the darn thing fixed last week, and already it's not working."*

*"Do you mind if I take a look at it? I own a shop about a quarter mile from here. Maybe it's something I can do to help,"* I said.

*"Well, I ain't got that much money. I spent my last bit of change tonight preparing for this storm that's about to hit. Anyways, I really don't like to depend on strangers, ya know. I'll call a friend and see if I can have him come and pick me up. But thanks anyway,"* she replied.

*"It'll be no problem. I can drop you off and come back for your car with my truck, and tow it to the shop. It'll cost you nothing but a smile, little lady."*

She stood there smiling. She introduced herself as Linda and I helped her transport her groceries from her car to mine. That night I dropped her off and went to the shop to get the tow truck, just like I said I would; and I towed her car back to the shop. Thankfully, the snow hadn't picked up yet, which gave me more than enough time to look at her engine.

The funny thing about the engine was, there wasn't anything *wrong* with it. When I looked under the hood, I noticed there was a piece of cloth tangled in it. I chalked it off to maybe, the mechanic she had spoken of earlier, had let his cloth tearing under the hood by mistake.

I used my knife to untangle the cloth. I then did a test run of the car, and all was well. I attached the car to the back of the tow truck and proceeded to Linda's house. I parked the tow truck in front of the house and walked up to the door. I noticed the door was slightly open. I called out to her to let her know I was back with her car, and that everything was fine. I turned the knob, knocked again, and let myself in.

*"Linda, it's me, Tony. I have your car, parked outside. The engine is fine. It just had a piece of cloth caught up in it."*

I walked into the living room and almost slipped. I looked down and noticed blood on the floor—blood I just slid in. That's when I first noticed the finger prints on the corner of the door, bloody fingerprints. My mind told me to run and get out of there as fast as I could, but my legs felt as if they had weights on them, like someone tied me down. I froze in panic; I couldn't believe what I had walked into.

I looked to my right and there she was—lying on the floor, clothes soaked in blood, groceries still in bags on the kitchen table. Her eyes were wide open, those beautiful hazel eyes now dark and dull. She was blue, she was dead. I could see where her throat had been slashed; and her mouth was wide open as if she had been calling out for help. Tear stains dried up on the side of her face.

*Who would do this?* I asked myself.

The next thing I knew, there were sirens, police sirens—lots of them. The next words I heard were: *"This is the police. Place your hands where I can see them."*

That was twenty-five years ago.

Twenty-five years ago, I stood as an innocent man. However, the prosecutor was able to win over the jury with theatrics, by playing on the emotions of the nine women who were in the jury. Here I was going to jail for a crime I didn't commit, for someone I didn't know. It's funny how things can change in the blink of an eye.

Years and years of appeals went unheard and unanswered. I felt hopeless. As faithful as I was in church, no one had come to testify on my behalf, or even visit me since I had been wrongfully accused. My mama and sister were the only two who supported me. At every court case and at every parole, I could count on mama and baby sis to be there for me.

However, all that changed last year when mama died and baby sis was diagnosed with cervical cancer. After going to mama's funeral in chains and seeing the stares from the mourners who attended, hearing the whispers and murmurs, I broke down. These people whom I knew since I was knee-high to a chicken; and now they looked at me with disgust and condemnation.

Six months after mama died, I received a letter that baby sis went home to be with the Lord. My attorney sent me the letter. I wasn't able to go to baby sis' funeral because the warden said I was allowed to go to only one funeral within a calendar year. I had used that allowance when mama died.

In the letter from the attorney were papers stating that all of mama's and baby sis' assets would be signed over to me. I thought: What good would this do me, if I stayed locked up in this prison?

While in prison, I prayed daily. I didn't understand how the Lord could allow all this to happen to me. But I knew for certain He'd bring me out. I joined the prison ministry team and held prayer meetings. But it was something about the other prisoners: They couldn't believe that I was innocent; and if I were guilty, they didn't believe that a convicted murder could change. I felt as if my past was on my back and the whole world could see it.

In some cultures, if an individual was accused of murder, the townspeople would tie the victim to the back of the accused until the corpse began to rot. With the victim tied to the back of the accused, everyone in the town would know what crime the accused was charged with, whether you were guilty or not. They didn't care because the evidence showed differently. The evidence showed that you were tried by a jury of your peers and the vote was unanimous—you were *guilty*!

I stood on those prison grounds feeling as if I was guilty,

even though I knew I hadn't done anything wrong. If I was guilty of anything, it wouldn't be of being in the wrong place at the wrong time. I was supposed to be where I was when I was, because I had a purpose for being there. However, the enemy, the devil, prowls around like a roaring lion looking for someone to devour; and so I happened to be his prey.

I felt like a sheep considered for slaughter. No matter what it is I faced while serving my time in prison, there were days that, like Job, I wish I hadn't been born. There were many nights I cried, *"May the night be wiped away when people said, 'A boy is born!'"* That was twenty-five years ago.

One day while in the prison library and studying Biblical numerology, tears swelled up in my eyes because I learned that the number seven represented *completion*; that it was God's perfect number, that it meant it was *finished!* And that it was *the end of time!*

While sitting behind those prison walls, thinking about life as I knew it, a part of me wanted to give up, but a part of me kept hanging on. Every night for twenty-five years, before I slept, I quoted Psalm 35:21-23:

> *"They open wide their mouths against me; they say, 'Aha, Aha! Our eyes have seen it!' You have seen, O Lord; be not silent! O Lord, be not far from me! Awake and rouse yourself for my vindication, for my cause, my God and my Lord!"*

Oh, how things can change in the blink of an eye. That was twenty-five years ago. I awoke to much noise and cheers. I wondered what could be going on today that was so different from the rest of the nine thousand, one hundred and thirty-two days I had spent behind these bars.

I looked up and saw my lawyer who, twenty-five years ago, took my case on for free. The same lawyer who traveled up and down the road for a convicted murder. The same lawyer who stood by my mother's side until she died. The same lawyer who made sure that my sister was put away well and that her affairs were in order. The same lawyer who didn't treat me like the number written across my prison-issued uniform. This was the lawyer I would learn to call—*friend*.

*"William, what are you doing this early in the morning?" I asked him.*

As the prison guard opened my cell, William said, *"Here, get dressed,"* tossing me a garment bag.

Inside the garment bag were a brand new suit, a white shirt and an Armani tie. I asked him what was with the suit and tie; and he replied with a smile, *"You have a court date, my friend."*

*A court date?* I looked over at the calendar on my prison wall which hung next to a copy of Psalm 35. I looked up at him and said, *"There's nothing stating I have a court date this morning, William. I'm sorry you came all the way up here, man, but you have your dates mixed up."*

I handed him back the garment bag and its contents.

*"So you mean to tell me that you've gotten so used to being in this place that you want to spend the rest of your life here?"* He asked.

*"What do you mean? What is it that you're saying to me?"* I asked him with tears in my eyes, not noticing that they were now falling down my face.

William updated me on my case. Six months ago, someone was arrested for murdering a young woman with brown hair and hazel eyes. When the man was arrested, they of course took his fingerprints. When they ran his fingerprints in the system, they matched the fingerprints that were left on the wall at the crime scene at Linda's house twenty-five years earlier.

My lawyer told me that the DNA that was taken from the man and the DNA found in Linda's rape kit were a match. They *never* mentioned that Linda had been *raped.* They did not have the DNA twenty-five years ago that they have today. *I was a free man!*

He said he didn't want to tell me anything until he knew *for sure* that everything was going to work out on my behalf. The story I gave twenty-five years ago proved correct. It so happened that the mechanic left his cloth on purpose! He was hoping to get to the mart to see her stranded so that he'd be the one to offer her a ride. But when he'd gotten back and saw her drive off with me, he'd become enraged by jealousy, waited for me to drop her off.

When I drove away, he walked into her home, raped her and then slashed her throat.

The neighbor next door heard her screams for help. When I got there the police were right behind me and automatically assumed that I was the murderer.

I walked out of the courtroom a free man that day. The wait was over and the weight that was tied to my back had been lifted. No more *stares* and no more *tears*. I was a walking testimony of Psalm 91:4:

*"He will cover you with his feathers, and under His wings you will find refuge;*

His faithfulness will be your shield and buckler."

| The Word: |
|---|

- Genesis 2:2
- Job 3:3
- Isaiah 54:17
- Proverbs 11:9
- Psalm 35:21-23
- Psalm 73
- Psalm 91:4
- Psalm 119:71
- Matthew 5:11
- Romans 8:36
- Romans 12:19

- 1 Peter 5:8
- Revelation 10:5, Revelation 16:17

## The Prayer:

"Father, in the Name of Jesus, O how Wonderful is Your Name. You are my Shield and Buckler! You are my Vindication against my accusers. You are ever Merciful and True; and though the righteous suffer, Yahweh, I know that the end of the wicked will be terrible!

It was good for me to be afflicted that I may learn of thy statutes. I acquired my wounds as worship unto You, O Lord, my God, my Redeemer. In Jesus Name, I thank You, and I give You praise! Amen!"

# LET IT GO – IT DOESN'T BELONG TO YOU

As day turned into night, Jonathan knew once the lights went out, the dreams would come again. He dreaded the night-time hours. He knew the nightmares would be dreadful, followed by night sweats and the occasional wetting the bed.

He wasn't accustomed to sleeping alone at night. Since he'd turned five years-old his dad no longer worked the late shift. Jonathan had now been sent to his room every night. No longer able to share the bed with his mother. Something that he had gotten used to. He loved his father, but he was angry with him, now that he had to sleep alone.

Jonathan's mother, Anna, purchased a stuffed teddy bear for him at the local toy store. She told him whenever he felt alone or afraid to hug the teddy bear and it would calm and help him go to sleep. Needless to say, since she brought the stuffed bear home – the bear she called Oscar – he had more than his share of restless nights and no matter how many times he hugged and squeezed Oscar, the nightmares kept happening.

Every other night Jonathan would be awakened by his parents arguing, which normally followed his mother's cries. His father belittled her and slapped her often.

Jonathan's hate grew towards his father. *Why wouldn't his father go back to work at night or just leave all together?* Jonathan asked himself. He and his mother were doing fine without him being there. When he did show up, he was his usual drunk self. Jonathan knew that whenever his father came home drunk, that there would be routine fights. He never understood why his mother put up with the abuse and why she had been so timid. He vowed that he'd kill his father if he hurt his mother again.

Anna came into Jonathan's room to wish him a good night, as she always had. However, this time when she came in, she had tears in her eyes. She kept telling him how much she loved him. *"I love you Jay. Mama's little man. Remember, if you ever start to feel alone or afraid, all you have to do is hug Oscar and he'll make all your fears disappear, alright."*

That night she kissed Jonathan on his forehead and handed Oscar the stuffed bear back to him. She tucked him in, turned off the lights and closed the door behind her. The next morning Jonathan awoke to the sound of dishes and pots thrown to the floor. He was too afraid to get out of his bed to see what all the commotion was about, so he pulled the covers up over his head and hoped that the big bad man that was destroying the house wouldn't come into his room and find him.

He laid in his room and hugged Oscar, hoping the sheets and blanket would make him invisible. He heard the door to his bedroom open. He felt the sheets and blankets as they were pulled off of him. So much for being invisible. So much for Oscar keeping him safe. No one could keep him safe from the big bad man he knew as dad, nobody but Anna, his mother – *where was she?*

*"Get up, you little sissy! Give me that damn toy! You're too big for a damn doll! I ain't raising no punks in this house! Where's ya mama? Where did she say she was going? Answer me boy! Don't just sit there looking like a got damn mute!"* his father said.

*"I don't know where ma – ma – mama, wha – wha – went – pop – poppa."* Jonathan stammered.

When Jonathan was born, he was diagnosed with a nervous condition which caused him to stutter when he spoke—a condition that irritated his father to no end. He hated that he had a son with a disability. He felt as if it made him less of a man. He often blamed Anna for Jonathan's deficient nervous system.

Anna saw that Jonathan wasn't growing at the same pace of a child his age should be. This concerned her. She took Jonathan to his primary doctor, who referred him to a speech therapist. At first they thought Jonathan may be autistic. After running several tests, it was apparent he had difficulties in producing speech in a normal fashion. His speech was haltered and fragmented. His speech was frequented with interruptions and difficulties producing words without effort or struggle.

Every time Jonathan tried to talk, his speech was haltered. His father, Marcus, would yell at him, which caused his issue to worsen. Because Jonathan feared his father, whenever Marcus came around, Jonathan would have nervous fits. He knew either Marcus was going to yell at him or, in frustration – hit him.

Whenever Anna was around she kept Jonathan away from Marcus. She'd often keep him in his room occupied with toys and books. When Jonathan got old enough for school she thanked God. That meant while Marcus was sleeping during the day, Jonathan would be in school. Since Marcus lost his job at the Navy Yard, he became increasingly difficult to deal with, abusive and an alcoholic.

Days turned into nights and nights turned into day. Still Anna had not returned home. Jonathan's stomach growled and ached. Marcus was too busy drinking to buy food and cook.

Jonathan cried himself to sleep many nights. There was no Oscar to hold anymore. Marcus took the stuffed bear and ripped it to shreds, daring Jonathan to shed a tear. Marcus told Jonathan for every tear he cried over the disfigured bear he would strike him with his belt. Jonathan sat refusing to cry. He refused to give his father the satisfaction of seeing his pain. However, that didn't keep Jonathan from crying at night – when he was left alone.

Late one night Jonathan looked out his window watching his father drive off. The further his father drove, the more Jonathan cried. He wondered if his father would come back or would he leave him the same as Anna, his mother had. He sat in the window with tears in his eyes, trying to remember the prayer he and Anna would say every night before she tucked him in...

> *"Now I lay me down to sleep,*
> *I pray the Lord my soul to keep,*
> *If I should die before I wake,*
> *I pray the Lord my soul to take.*
> *Amen."*

Every morning, Marcus would return. However, Anna did not. Year after year, day after day, Jonathan prayed that prayer. He also prayed that his mother would come back home. He didn't care where she'd been or why she left, all he wanted was his mother. The older Jonathan got, the image of his dear mother Anna, began to fade from his memory.

Marcus removed every trace of Anna from the house, as if she never existed. The only way Jonathan was able to keep her image alive was to sneak into his father's room, go under his bed and find his father's old photo album. He sat on the bedroom floor and pretend to have conversations with his mother. Every day it was some-thing different to talk about. He'd talk about school and or some girl he was fancy for. He'd ask her advice and then reply to himself, saying, *"Mama's little man – you know there ain't no girl good enough for mama's baby."*

Time passed, and Jonathan didn't hear Marcus come in. Marcus walked into his room and there Jonathan was, having one of his imaginary conversations with Anna's picture. Marcus walked over to him and slapped Jonathan across the face, yelling and belittling him, as he'd always done. He called Jonathan a retarded sissy that no woman in her right mind would want. He was nothing but a stuttering, disabled fool.

Jonathan sat on the floor and refused to cry. He sat there with his heart hardened against the big bad man. Marcus knew that names and physical abuse no longer fazed Jonathan, so he took his cigarette lighter out of his back pocket and set Anna's pictures on fire.

Jonathan, no longer the five-year-old boy, stood and tried to snatch the pictures from the flames. But it was too late. Little by little, he saw the flame consume his mother's image, the same way his mother's image would fade away in years to come.

Marcus remarried and had other children. Marcus and his new wife Tracey kept Jonathan in the garage of their new home. In the back of the garage, was a makeshift room for him and they fed him through the door of the garage. Tracey and Marcus wouldn't let his other brothers and sisters engage with him. Jonathan felt alone and ashamed of his disability. He resented God and no longer prayed the prayer his mother taught him. He resented her too. She abandoned him and left him to suffer alone.

As Jonathan got older, he finished school. He wasn't allowed to attend his prom or any parties. He had no friends and was often bullied. He made up in his mind he was going to leave that garage and the big bad man behind.

That summer, Jonathan ran away. He waited until the middle of the night when he knew all would be asleep. He took one of the suitcases his stepmother kept in the basement, and packed what little belongings he had. He left not knowing where he'd end up, but anywhere was better than where he was. That night he walked the streets until dawn.

As Jonathan traveled through the night into dawn he heard noises coming from the woods. He wondered *who could be making so much noise this time of morning.* The curiosity in him wanted to go and check out what the noise could be, but his fear and timidity kept him at a standstill.

*"Are you okay sir?"* came the voice of a young woman from behind him, which startled him.

Jonathan turned to see a beautiful young lady staring back at him. It was then he heard the haunting voice of his father, Marcus echoing in his ear, *"ain't no woman in her right mind gonna want a retarded sissy, much less a stuttering, disabled fool."* Jonathan looked at the young lady and wouldn't mumble a word.

*"Well, Jessica and I are on our way back into the camp meeting. Our church is having a tent revival all week. The Lord's been blessing us real good. My name is Julia. What's your name?"* She asked.

Jonathan stood there with his hands behind his back, head down looking at his shoes, too afraid to speak for fear he'd embarrass himself. Just then, the little girl

Jessica took his hand, saying, *"Mister, don't be scared, we won't hurt you. Here, take this, this is what I hold on to when I'm afraid."*

She pulled from behind her a stuffed teddy bear. *"You can hold him,"* she said, *but you'll have to give him back. His name is Oscar."*

Jonathan looked at the little girl, tears streaming down his face. In the eyes of the little girl he saw someone familiar. He saw his mother – he saw *Anna.*

*"Don't cry, mister,"* said the little girl. *"You can keep Oscar if you want. Whenever you're afraid or alone, just hold on to him and he'll help you get through all your fears,"* she continued.

*"Well, we best be going. We'll be here for two more days. If you want to join us, we'd be more than glad to have you,"* Julia said.

Julia then took Jessica by the hand and went back into the campgrounds to join the others – without Oscar, the teddy bear. That night Jonathan stayed next to the camp, close by the highway where the revival was going on. Julia saw him, and brought him a plate of food, along with a blanket to cover himself from the night winds.

Jonathan lay on the side of the highway that night. Holding Oscar, the stuffed teddy bear in his arms, he closed his eyes and drifted fast asleep. Jonathan had a dream...

"Hello, Jonathan, do you mind if I take that bear?"
"No, this is my bear and you can't have him!"
said Jonathan.
"You have to let it go in order to grow."
"No, I'm not ready to let go of my bear, he's mine!"
said Jonathan.
"No Jonathan, Oscar's not yours. He belongs to
someone else."
"No, mama gave him to me. She told me whenever I was
alone or afraid to hug him. And right now, I'm alone and
afraid and he's all I have!" said Jonathan.
"Jonathan, I promise you – you are not alone. Trust me.
All you have to do is hand Oscar over to me.
I promise you, I won't leave you."
"I can't, he belongs to me, and I can't let him go!
He was already taken from me once, and I won't let
that happen to me again," said Jonathan.
"But Jonathan, don't you want to experience true love?
Come on, give that hurt to me."
"No, this hurt is mine!" said Jonathan.
"Give me that anger you're holding on to."
"No, I don't want to let it go. You can't make me,"
said Jonathan.
"I know you're hurting and confused, but I can make it
all go away. All you have to do is trust me."
"I can't, I can't trust you. It hurts too much to trust,"
said Jonathan.
"You can, Jonathan. You can trust me.
Look at what it is you're holding.
Look at Oscar again, now, tell me, what it is you see?"

Jonathan looked down at the stuffed animal, only this time he didn't recognize it. What he saw was his emotions – emotions that kept him imprisoned all those years. For the first time he was able to see the fear, the loneliness, the abandonment, the anger, hurt and low self-esteem he'd carried. Jonathan, now seeing things differently, lifted up the stuffed bear; and in his dream, he saw the hands of God take it away.

Jonathan walked into the tent the following morning as the saints were in prayer. They embraced him, and he knew from that day on he would no longer be bound by fear, loneliness, abandonment, anger, hurt of brokenness. He found a new family – he found *God's* love.

| The Word: |
|:---:|

- Psalm 127:3-5
- Psalm 139:13-16
- Proverbs 22:6
- Deuteronomy 31:6
- Joshua 1:9
- Song of Solomon 4:7
- 2 Chronicles 7:14
- Exodus 14:14
- Micah 7:8
- James 1:20
- Ephesians 6:1-4

## The Prayer:

"Abba Father, my heart is wounded and I am broken. I feel forsaken and alone. Many are my wounds and sorrows! Please, help me – heal me. You promised me that You'd never leave me, nor forsake me, that You would be with me always, even until the end of the ages. You said that You've written my name on the backs of Your hands, that I'm never out of Your sight. I take refuge in knowing that I am Your child and that I am not forgotten.

In Jesus' Name. Amen."

# BUT I WAITED

Walking out of New Hope Cathedral, Vanessa was the happiest woman in the world. She felt that life was finally coming together for her just as she had planned. She believed in the principles of God's words and she was a stickler for Proverbs 18:22: *"He who finds a wife finds a good thing and obtains favor from the Lord."*

All of her life Vanessa was taught by her mother, Elect-Lady Mildred Price; and her father, the Most Reverend Eli Price, that she was a *good thing* and that she was some man's *favor.* She was taught to make sure she kept herself pure and above reproach. Her parents taught her that God had her Boaz waiting somewhere for her; and she *was waiting* to be found. That's what she did: she waited and at forty-two years old, she found her *"Boaz."*

As Vanessa and her new husband, *Elliott,* made their way down the steps of the New Hope Cathedral, the church in which she grew up, she took time to thank the smiling well-wishers who stood at the bottom of the stairs, yelling their various congratulations while throwing rice at them.

She was glad that she *waited*, because Elliott was all the man she could ever hope for. He was fine, he had a chocolate complexion with pearly white teeth. As she could see from the looks of his physique, he was well-built.

Not only that, but he was an entrepreneur and a successful one at that. He made well over a six-figure salary. So she knew that they'd always be taken care of. She did grow up as the only daughter of a prestigious bishop; and she wouldn't have settled for anything less.

While the other girls in the church had experienced life, she was all too afraid to do the same. Some of those very girls she befriended at New Hope Cathedral had become teen mothers, drug addicts, unkempt. Her best friend was a lesbian. Vanessa was so glad that she didn't get caught up as they had.

However, it wasn't as if she wasn't curious in things like smoking weed and having oral sex. She knew that she couldn't get pregnant doing that; but still, she didn't. Her mother always told her, *"Baby, God has an all-seeing eye and He can see what I can't!"* Now that she looked back on her upbringing, it wasn't God whom she feared, it was her parents.

At forty-two years old, she wondered if she'd ever be able to conceive a child. She knew that time was against her. Even though her brother and his wife had several children, she wanted a child of her own. She loved being an aunt for her brother's children; however, she wanted a child of her own. She wanted to be a mother just as badly as she wanted to be a wife.

That is what Vanessa envied the most about the other women in the church. Yes, some had premarital sex. Yes, some had a baby or two out of wedlock. But no matter how they conceived their child, year after year, baby shower after baby shower, christening after christening, she stood there at New Hope Cathedral's altar with a false smile on her face.

Every time she witnessed one or the other, she selfishly wished it had been she. She had to be honest with herself; there were times when she thought she'd never get the chance to say "I do" or to hear the doctor say, *"It's a boy"* or *"it's a girl."*

Oh, how she longed to hear the latter. She knew that she and Elliott would make great parents. He'd come from a good Christian upbringing and she knew he'd be a wonderful dad. She made a mental note to start working on her family as soon as possible.

At one point in her life, Vanessa didn't care if she was the *Bishop's daughter.* At times her heart told her, *"Just do it!"* Others had done it, and while they remained the gossip of the church for a while, eventually things died down and the people moved on to other things to frown upon. But now today was *her* big day and she was glad *she waited.*

The next three months were everything she could ever dream. She married the man she always hoped for. When they made love for the first time, she knew that it was something that she would be doing often. Something told her that it wasn't his first time. But it was certainly hers, and he made *every* nerve in her body come alive. She wanted to feel that feeling over and over and over again.

She sometimes sat in church smiling from ear to ear.

Everyone told her how happy she looked and how happy they were for her. If those sanctified sisters knew why she was smiling so much, they would have had a conniption. Often times, while her father was in the peak of his sermon she'd be daydreaming about Elliott and what they did the night before. Before she knew it, she'd be up on her feet shouting, *"Yes! Yes!"*

Vanessa learned earlier on from her mother that when a preacher is long-winded, one must get up and encourage him to bring the message to a close. She couldn't wait for her father to bring this message to a close, for the altar call to be completed or the benediction to be given. She wanted to go home and be with her husband. Tonight she had her own *services* planned for her and Elliott. There would be no encouragement to bring that service to a close. She would let him hold *service* for as long as he wanted.

She remembered what her grandmother, Mother Helen, told her: *"Don't you take no advice from none of these single women in here, ya' hear! That's why they's single. Not even ya mama."* Mother Helen paused, to take a look around to see if anyone was listening, before she said, *"If ya ask me, she a little frigid. She got a icebox where her snatch used ta be.*

*"Listen, honey, your mama may not have had the talk with you. But you a married woman now, and if you want ta keep 'em, you gotta learn how to pray in the church and lay in ya bedroom. Don't ever get the two mixed up! 'Cause Jesus ain't coming to keep ya warm at*

*night; and ya can't make love to him. That big ole choco-*
*late thing over there, ya better drop it like it's hot on him*
*e'er chance you's get.*

*"If I was a little younger and didn't have this catheter*
*up in me, I'd give you a run for ya money and take ya*
*honey. But these days the only thing I'm running for is*
*the bathroom," she said laughing.* "Remember, Paul said
*in Corinthians, that a wife should satisfy her husband's*
*sexual desires; and that yo body ain't your-ons. It be-*
*longs to him and he belongs to you.'*

Well, that advice paid off. Six months later, Vanessa
found out she was pregnant. She and her best friend
Angela started planning the baby shower and register-
ing online at different outlets.

Vanessa was excited. She knew that children were a gift
from God. She planned on being the best mother she
could be. God had blessed her womb; and she knew,
like Hannah, when their baby turned a year old, they'd
stand before New Hope Cathedral and give him back to
the Lord.

Things were going as expected. She found love and she
learned to love. She was three months along in her pregnancy and it showed. She had a very happy pregnancy
so far. She even thanked God for the morning sickness—
she was so excited. She supervised the painting of the
nursery and picked colors and accents as well as furniture and clothing. She looked online and in catalogues,
all the while beaming with happiness. She thought how
cute the little clothes were and how they would look on
her bundle of joy.

While sitting at the table in their formal dining room, she was startled when the phone rang. She yelled up to Elliott that she would get the phone; but when she picked up he had already answered. Before she could hang up, the voice on the other end held her attention. She listened carefully with her hands covering her mouth, and tried to hold in her cries. Just as she started to weep, the phone disconnected.

There she stood in the middle of her dining room. Her emotions were heightened and she didn't know what to think, much less what to say. When was he going to tell me? She was afraid. She was hoping what she heard, she really didn't hear. Why!! She demanded *to know* to one in particular.

Why was this happening to *her, to them?* After all, she'd done everything she was supposed to do—she *waited.* Now, all that she waited so long for was threatened to be taken away.

All she could do was cry. She held her belly and she cried for what was to come. When was Elliott going to tell her that he had been diagnosed with Non-Hodgkin's Lymphoma?

She overheard the doctor saying that the test had come back and that he needed to come in right away. But Elliott told the doctor that he was too tired to come in, and that he would be all right whether the news was good or bad. He could take it, just tell him. After Elliott gave these assurances, his doctor let him know that the treatments weren't working and that the outcome was grim.

That explained it all. It explained the fevers, sudden weight loss and loss of appetite. It explained the restless nights and early mornings. Why was he home more often than usual, helping her to pick out things for the baby—his baby—he *knew!*

Elliott made his way down the stairs. Looking at him, one would say he still seemed healthy. He just looked like someone who'd lost a few pounds. He called out to Vanessa. She wiped her eyes. He told her he needed to talk to her about something of importance and that it was urgent. She replied with a barely audible *'okay.'* When he made it to the bottom of the stairs he took one look at her and he knew. SHE KNEW.

Right there, at the bottom of the stairs with no words spoken, they embraced. They wept. They consoled one another. She took her hands and laid them on her husband. Right then and there she knew that the honeymoon was over; and if her husband had any chance of defying the odds, she would have to call on all the heavenly host.

She knew that she'd have to call on the prayer warriors at the church. Most of all, she'd have to call on her grandmother and the Mothers' Board. She knew from experience, if anybody could get a prayer through to God, the *mothers* could.

Weeks and months went by; and the saints sent up prayers. Day and night the prayers of the righteous went up before the Lord. With the prayers going up and the deterioration of her husband, Vanessa felt like she was fighting a losing battle. She lost hope. The doctors had given Elliott a few months to life, which was better than the few weeks they had given him prior.

She was due a month from now. She was afraid and inconsolable. She was *angry with God*. This is not what she *waited for*. She was *angry* with those women who had children and husbands. She was also *angry* with the men who didn't take care of their wives and children; those are the people she felt should be going through this, not her. She wept and she wailed, because she waited and now everything was turning out *wrong.*

As she stood in her kitchen, surrounded by some of the intercessors who had been over to the house, her water broke. It looked like the baby was coming early. She stood, holding onto a chair when her mother came running over to her. She looked at her mother and said that she wasn't ready to have the baby, that the baby was too early; that Elliott was still in the hospital.

*"He promised me, ma! Elliott promised me that he'd be here when the baby was born, he promised!"* Vanessa cried. But her mother reminded her that God's timing was not man's timing, and that the baby wasn't going to wait any longer. She was going to call the ambulance and take her daughter.

While Vanessa and her mother waited for the EMT to take them to the hospital, the home phone rang. It was the hospital calling to tell her if she wanted to say her goodbyes that she would need to get to there immediately. Out of nowhere, Elliott had taken a turn for the worse. Just like her mother just told her, *God's timing was not like men's.*

When God was ready to bring one of his children home, there wasn't anything anyone could do. No matter how much they prayed and believed for a miracle, it was now in God's hand, and it was up to Him, and Him alone, to decide.

Once the ambulance reached St. Mary's Hospital, they immediately ushered Vanessa to the delivery ward on the second floor. Something had gone horribly wrong. She was suddenly short of breath and she could feel herself drifting in and out of consciousness. The last thing she heard was the doctors say to the nurse in the room, *"If we don't take this baby now, we may lose both the mother and the child."*

Vanessa was told she had a condition called *Eclampsia* when she went for a checkup. The doctor told her that her blood pressure was elevated and she needed to take antihypertensive drugs. But with the diagnosis given to Elliott just months before, she had totally neglected to follow up with her appointments. She spent most—if not all—of her time at the hospital with Elliott at his doctor appointments.

With the baby coming earlier than expected, and Elliott just floors above fighting for his life, Vanessa found herself in a dangerous situation. The doctors were able to keep her calm while her mother prayed and walked the room. Vanessa wept as she lay there in that hospital bed waiting to give birth, and breathing as she had been taught in her Lamaze Class. Oh, how she wished her husband were there with her. Vanessa's mother came over to hold her hand. *"Vanessa, there's someone on the phone who wants to speak with you,"* she said.

Vanessa looked at her mother as if she had lost her mind. Here she was, in the hospital, giving birth and worrying about her beloved, and someone had the audacity to call her? How *inconsiderate,* she thought, while rolling her eyes at her mother. Her mother stood up and placed the phone to Vanessa's ear against her protest.

*"Hey, Bay,"* came the faint voice on the other end. The voice she came to love. The voice whose deep baritone hugged her heart each time it spoke. Now that thunderous voice was just above a whisper. It was Elliott's voice. *"How's my baby holding up?"* He asked. It took everything in Vanessa to keep from breaking down. *"I must be strong,"* she thought to herself.

*"Your baby is about to come any minute now, E. I wish you...I'm glad you're here with me, baby. I can't do this without you,"* she said.

*"Yes you can, Bay. You're strong, and we're in this together. You know I love you! Now we're going to get through this together. I'm going to be on the phone with you until our lil man is born,"* Elliott said.

*"How do you know it's a boy?"* She asked.

*I asked the Lord, if I didn't live to see my baby born what would it be?* He replied. They both now were crying silently in each other's ears. *"The Lord spoke to my heart*

159

*and said, 'A boy,' and that's when I knew it'll be okay,*
*Bay. The Lord said the baby would be a boy and I want*
*us to name him after me—Elijah Elliott Earhart."*

Elliott never did like his first name, Elijah, until one day
when Vanessa's father was preaching the story about
Elijah and the widow woman. Bishop Price was in the
middle of his preaching and told the congregation that
Elijah's name means *"My God is Yahweh!"* That morning, he preached a sermon titled *"My God IS God."*

After that sermon, Elliott no longer disliked his first
name. He wanted to be called Eli or Elijah. He said that
his name had found meaning. He wanted their son to
be proud of his name. Vanessa often teased him about
what if the baby was a girl. He'd look at Vanessa and
said, 'Well, then, we'll name her *Widow.* We'd then
both laugh, not knowing how prophetic that would be
months later. Me, Vanessa Danielle Price-Earhart, the
*widow* of Elijah Elliott Earhart, and *mother* to Elijah
Elliott Earhart, Jr.

After speaking with Elliott, she knew deep down in her
heart she'd be okay with whatever *the Lord's will.* Two
hours, fourteen minutes and thirteen seconds later,
Vanessa gave birth to their precious baby boy. After
preparing her and baby Elijah, she and the new bundle
of joy were escorted upstairs to the hospice care unit.
Vanessa laid baby Elijah on his father's chest.

While Elliott prayed for his newborn son, and he and
his brave wife held hands. Baby Elijah lay in his arms,
as the Lord called him home. Though she was overcome

with grief, Vanessa was able to smile, because as always, Elliott kept his promise—*he waited.*

---
## The Word:
---

- 1 Samuel 2:20
- Ruth 2:5
- Ecclesiastes 4:9-12
- Psalm 23
- Psalm 90:12
- Psalm 116:15
- Psalm 127:3
- Proverbs 1:7
- Proverbs 16:9
- Proverbs 18:22
- Proverbs 19:20
- Proverbs 22:6
- Jeremiah 20:17-18
- John 14:1-3
- Romans 12:2
- 1 Corinthians 7:4-14
- 1 Corinthians 10:13
- James 4:13-14

---
## The Prayer:
---

"Father, Your Word declares, *'Precious in the sight of the Lord is the death of his faithful servants.'* Sometimes I don't understand what Your plan is for my life. You are a God who is too big to make a mistake. Your will is good, it is acceptable and it is perfect. Teach me how to number my days. Teach me how to embrace my now, while I let go of my then. Teach me how to love beyond my hurt and live above my fears. Teach me how to understand that what I have is borrowed—this body, this soul, this spirit, this breath and even this time. It's all borrowed and it all belongs to You. In Jesus' Name. Amen."

# THE GIFT WITHOUT
# THE GIVER

Norman walked in his front door. The first thing he did was pick up the remote and turn on the evening news. He barely got his coat and shoes off before he flopped down on his favorite chair to hear the latest news.

He'd just gotten in from his sister's house, having Sunday dinner with her family, when suddenly he realized that he needed to get home before the news.

He could very well have watched the news over at his sister's house. But with all of the noise and running around her children did, he knew that he would be frustrated if he stayed one more second. Plus, his favorite artist would be interviewed during the news segment and he didn't want to miss it.

When the news went to commercial break, Norman went to his kitchen, grabbed a beer and some snacks. After the commercial, his favorite singer would be interviewed and then give the performance of a lifetime. Norman never really did understand what people meant when they said they would be giving *a performance of a lifetime*, but he didn't care.

He knew that Aubrey could sing—and sing well. She was untouchable and confident, humble and meek; yet when she opened her mouth to sing, she commanded the room. No doubt she was an up-and-coming superstar with a presence and poise that could not be denied.

Norman smiled to himself, thinking not too long ago, him and his wife Angelique had sent their baby girl off to school. She had graduated from high school and went straight to college with a dream of becoming a prosecutor.

However, once she started college and joined the choir, her interest soon changed. She called home and told her parents she no longer wanted to be a prosecutor, she wanted to be a singer.

He and Angelique thought she'd lost her mind, and Angelique wouldn't have her daughter become nobody's singer. Angelique told her they didn't send her to college to become somebody's five-and-dime night club act. If she didn't get back into her studies, Angelique was going to come up to that college and drag her behind right back to New Orleans.

It had taken them years to save up for a college education for their one and only daughter. Their son David already got a scholarship to Howard U and was well on his way to becoming the professional they always dreamed he would be. But their baby girl; well, she was all together something different. She had defiance in her that would make you want to kill her.

Sometimes he and Angelique would blame one another, saying that she got her stubborn will from his or her family, depending on what she had done.

Now, sitting on his couch, looking up at the picture over the fireplace of his beloved Angelique, he knew that his wife would be proud of their baby girl and what she had become.

Norman waited patiently as the commercials ended and the news resumed. He listened carefully as always. The interviewer asked Aubrey what inspired her the most.

Aubrey smiled and said with a twinkle in her eye, *"My parents—my parents have always been my inspiration. They have always been there for me, even when they did not agree with my choice of profession. You see, my parents had sent me away to college because at that time I'd wanted to study law. I wanted to be a prosecutor. My dream was to own the court system and prosecute the bad guy. But my dad, Norman is his name, hey daddy!"* she said, waving at the prompter, *"if you're watching, I love you!*

*"My dad always told me to follow my dreams no matter how silly they may seem to others."*

*Well, well, seems like you have a great father, Aubrey. What changed your mind from law school to wanting to be a singer? Give us a visual of that moment, the moment when you first realized you had that magic in your voice, that special sound that touched the hearts of people?* The interviewer asked.

*"Well, I always knew I could sing. I grew up in the church. At the age of five I sang my first song with the children's choir. We were called the HRC Youth Choir of the Holy*

165

*Redeemer Church of God in Christ. We had a wonderful choir directress; I believe Joyce was her name. She taught us this little simple song called J.E.S.U.S by this gospel group called the Winans. I believe they are brothers.*

*"Anyway, I remember hearing the song being played before rehearsal. By the time we started to learn it, I knew every riff and run. Joyce, the choir directress, asked me to lead it and I did. When I opened my mouth that Sunday morning, I could feel God's presence all over me. I saw people crying and throwing their hands up in the air giving God praise. I knew then, at that moment, I wanted to sing.*

*"However, as the years progressed, I stopped going to church. Though my parents still attended, I got a little older and decided church wasn't for me. But all that changed in my sophomore year. My friend Roger wanted to join the choir at the school and the brother really could sing. As a matter of fact, he's one of my background singers.*

*"Maybe, if he's not too shy, I can have him come out and wave at the camera,"* Aubrey said, smiling.

*"So Roger and I went to a rehearsal and I mean everybody could sing. They could really hold their own. I was immediately intimidated. I thought I was going to sing with some five-and-dime people, as my mother would call them. But, no sir, these people were sangers, not singers, but sangers."* She chuckled.

*"Roger challenged me to audition and when I finally did,*

*I was told I didn't pass the audition. I was laughed right out of the music room. I called my mother and cried and she showed me no mercy. After all, she didn't send me to college to be a singer, you know? She sent me there to practice law and that's what she expected me to do.*

*"Well honey, I cried, boo-hooted and belly ached for the next six months. Then I called my mother and told her I was going to be a singer, whether she liked it or not. She threatened to come up to my school and, in her words, drag me back to New Orleans, by the naps on the back of my neck if she had to. Unbeknownst to her, I auditioned for the choir again and this time I sang the roof off the room. There was no denying me membership. So I began to sing with the choir and continued with my studies as well."*

*Tell us, Aubrey, how did it all change for you?* The interviewer asked.

*"One-night Roger dared me to go with him to the amateur night in the hood, and we went. Once we arrived, he dared me to sing and I told him I would sing if he'd sing with me. That night we sang a song called Fire and Desire by Rick James and Tina Marie. There was in the audience an A&R, an Artist and Repertoire of Nehemiah Records scouting for talent. Here I am being interviewed by you. And the rest is history,"* said Aubrey.

*I know your mom was glad she didn't come and drag you back to New Orleans,* the interviewer said, laughing. *I know she has to be really proud of you. Let me see—six Grammy's and a number of other notable achievements,* he continued.

"Well, my mama was very glad she didn't come and drag me back to New Orleans. She was very proud of me. She passed away on Christmas Day last year from breast cancer. You know, she eventually supported me but she also said I was stubborn like my dad."

Norman looked up and spoke to his wife's picture, *"Oh you did—did ya? I told you, Angelique baby, the girl was stubborn like you. You lucky you got the entire heavenly host backing you up right now, because I'd come up to heaven and have a little talk with you and Jesus."* He laughed.

*Let me ask you one other question, Aubrey, before you perform tonight. What was it that made you stay a gospel artist all these years? I mean, with a voice such as yours, you could have done any other genre of music. Why gospel?* The interviewer asked.

"Well, first of all, I must say, that every good and perfect gift is from above," Aubrey replied. "I also want to say that I don't use the word perform. I like to say minister. I take what I do very seriously. If I never had Grammy's, Dove or Stellar Awards or any other form of recognition, I'd still do what I do.

"To answer your question, I chose to stay with gospel music, not because I was raised in the church. I chose to stick with it because I have such an undying love for the genre. It was because of what I saw when the Spirit of the Lord moves.

"You see; I couldn't sing about my baby or my man or getting laid. Now don't get me wrong, I love and listen *to all types of music, but I knew it wasn't for me. I knew that my gift is a responsibility. I also knew that my level of influence could cause others to come to Christ.*

*"I sing the gospel, not inspirational, not happy, feel-good music. I sing about the coming of Christ, about repentance, and His love and His judgments. "Ed,"* she acknowledged the interviewer.

*"The word of God says that the law of the Lord is perfect, converting the soul; the testimony of the Lord is sure, making wise the simple. In other words, the instruction of the Lord is perfect, renewing one's life, the testimony of the Lord is trustworthy, making the inexperienced wise,"* said Aubrey.

*"It is my duty to introduce God to the simple and the inexperienced. It is my job to keep God's commandments and to love everybody the way He tells me to, and to follow His instructions and plans for my life. If I testify of the Lord and live truly according to His word, then the inexperienced, the unknowing, the lost, the lame, the lowly, will all come to know this God, this Christ, this King, I serve and sing about.*

*"And before I go out to minister, I'd also like to say to the viewers, 'The gifts and calling of God are without repentance. It does not mean that God confers his favors on man without his exercising repentance, but that God does not repent, or change, in His purposes on bestowing His gifts on man. What He promises He will fulfill; what He purposes to do, He will not change from or repent of.'"*

169

*Wow, with that being said, let me introduce to some and present to others, Aubrey. Aubrey McDaniel's singing her new GRAMMY-nominated hit, "Calling Out to You..."*

Looking at the television with tears streaming down his face, Norman was grateful for the gift he and Angelique had been entrusted with. The gift they called Brea, the world had come to know as the voice, Aubrey. With hands lifted high, he waved them in praise to God, and with his mouth opened, Norman gave God high praises.

| The Word: |
|:---:|

- Psalm 19:7
- Psalm 98:1
- Psalm 149:6
- Proverbs 22:6
- Matthew 5:16
- Romans 12:3-11
- Romans 11:29
- 1 Corinthians 3:8
- 1 Corinthians 15:10
- James 1:7
- 1 John 2:15-17
- 1 Peter 4:10-11
- 1 Corinthians 12:4-6
- Proverbs 23:22
- Ephesians 6:7
- 2 Corinthians 9:12

## The Prayer:

"Father, in the Name of Jesus, I want to thank You for trusting me to be an ambassador for you. I will continue to let my light so shine so others can see my good work and glorify You who are in heaven. Thank you for this gift of voice, so that I can communicate through word and song the awesomeness of my God.

To tell a dying world that I serve a risen Savior and that You're in the world today. You are the living Savior, regardless of what men believe. It's because of Your mercy and voice of encouragement that I can go and live from day to day.

Thank You for sealing me with your Holy Spirit. Without Him, I can do nothing, but with Him I can do all things. In Jesus' Name I pray. Amen."

# COME OUT
# OF THE CORNER

I felt as if my life were over. I sat there wondering if this was my final curtain call. How would I be remembered? Would people care that I was no longer a part of this living, breathing society of individuals who, at some point in the mind of God, was created to live in this dispensation, at the same time, breathing the same air?

The more pain I felt, the more I wanted to just ball up in a corner. The voices in my head were loud and its tone overbearingly boisterous. "You are a failure!" "You'll never be anything!"

"Those people don't care about you; they are only using you!" The voices were threatening. I was very afraid.

There in the corner, I awoke, not knowing that I had fallen asleep. All I knew was I must have had another episode. The enemy was fighting to take my mind, my esteem and my peace.

But with everything in me, I refused to let him have the last say. I refused to be haunted by the rejection of yesterday and the words that haunted me daily. I refused to be a statistic, the latest topic of discussion over breakfast, lunch, dinner, over somebody's pulpit.

I could see the newspaper story about me, written in my mind as clear as day: *"ANOTHER PASTOR TAKES HIS LIFE."*

Can you imagine how I felt in the darkness of my room alone, no one to pray for me? At this point, I knew that if I was to survive, I would have to wait. When I say war—I mean just that—WAR! The pretty prayers wouldn't work this time. No rehearsed message or biblical knowledge would get me through this round of bullying from the devil. He was trying to *KILL ME.*

When we read the book of Ephesians, the scriptures tell us in chapter 6 that we wrestle not against flesh and blood, but against principalities, against powers, against the rulers of the darkness of this world, against spiritual wickedness in high places.

I was going through this not only in my head but I was going through it in my heart. I had to get ready to fight! Proverbs tells us to *"guard our hearts above all else, for it determines the course of our life."* The enemy kept speaking to me, telling me what the Lord had promised me would never come to pass. Like a fool, I believed him! I believed him because everything I tried to do, whether big or small, seemed to fall apart. People whom I trusted failed me big time. Through it all, I became weaker and weaker. My heart was broken.

In front of everyone, I was the little engine that could. But behind closed doors, I was a basket case. I'd totally forgotten Jeremiah's wisdom when he encouraged the believer:

*"Blessed is the man that trusts in the Lord, and whose hope is in the Lord...The heart is deceitful above all things, and desperately wicked; who can know it. It is the Lord who searches the heart of man and tries the reins..."* I'd lost focus.

Beloved, the Psalmist tells us, *"Put not your trust in princes, or in a son of man in whom there is no help."* I'd lost my focus on God because I placed my focus on the empty promises of man.

Isaiah, Chapter 31 narrates how the nation of Judah was facing the inevitable invasion from the mighty Assyrian army. There were counselors in King Hezekiah's court who were trying to get King Hezekiah to seek help from the Egyptians—which would have led to their doom.

They would have been doomed because they went down to Egypt thinking that horses could help them. They were impressed by the military mathematics and awed by the sheer number of chariots and riders—and to the Holy God of Israel they didn't even look, not even a glance, not so much as a prayer to God.

Still, He must be reckoned with, a most wise God who knows what He's doing. He can call down catastrophe. He's a God who does what He says. He intervenes in the work of those who do wrong, stands up against interfering evildoers. Egyptians are mortal, not God; and their horses are flesh, not Spirit.

When God gives the signal, helpers and helped alike will fall in a heap and share the same dirt grave.

I didn't get it! Egypt was a place of bondage! Why was I seeking help from a helpless people, when God already spoke and gave me a plan? I was trying to form an alliance with people to whom I wasn't supposed to be connected. I felt severely rejected when I was not accepted into the "who's who." I didn't understand that God had called me out—not called me in.

Whenever you are called by God for a specific task, it is God who makes the provision, pays the bill, wins the war, etc. When we try to do things on our own or when we try to connect to something that looks like God but is not, we sign ourselves over for fools' classes. Sometimes God *is* in a thing, yes. He has orchestrated and approved it. But does that mean you're supposed to be a part of it? *No!*

We execute plans—but they aren't of God. We form alliances—but not of God's Spirit, in order to add sin to sin. We take counsel and submit to coverings that are not of God. Then we become stubborn and eventually rebellious, and sometimes bitter. We think because these people have a multiplicity of funding and an unyielding support, that God has to be blessing them. And it isn't so.

I'd lost my focus because I'd lost my praise. I'd forgotten that *PRAISE WINS THE BATTLE—NOT THE PROVISIONS OF MEN.*

Isaiah confronted Judah with two sins that he noticed. The first sin was trusting in Egypt and their military might. The second sin was not looking unto the

Holy One of Israel. Judah felt that they had a reason to put their trust in these chariots because there were so many. Judah also felt they had a reason to put their trust in the horsemen because they were very strong. But they couldn't find a reason to place their trust in the Lord. They did not, of course, abandon their faith.

However, Jerusalem's leaders put their trust in Egypt. Everybody lives by faith, don't they? Yes. Financiers trust market forces. Militarists trust bombs. Scientists trust nature's regularities. But *faith* isn't the problem; *where* we put our faith in times of crisis—that's the problem.

The scriptures tell us that we walk by faith and not by sight. Just as the children of Israel, I began to look at the promises of men and what they could offer me, not realizing that if I'd just kept the faith in The Holy One of Israel, regardless as to what was being offered by man, then God would eventually bring to pass the provision. The word of God says that the cattle on a thousand hills belongs to Him, and the earth is the Lord's and the fullest thereof, the world and they that dwell therein.

Unlike the heart of the Psalmist in Psalm 20:7, *"Some trust in chariots, and some in horses; but we will remember the Name of the Lord our God,"* he that stands with one foot on a rock, and another upon a quicksand, will sink and perish as certainly as he that stands with both feet on quicksand.

I was double-minded and quickly sinking. I had let self-will come between me and God. God hadn't called me out from among them to remain friends. He called me out to fight against them. It seemed easier *to go along* than to *move alone.* Though Judah couldn't seem to find a reason to trust God, the reasons were there and Isaiah had to remind them.

There in the darkness of my mind, God began to remind me. He reminded me that He didn't call me to win a popularity contest, nor to have any names in bright lights one someone's marquee. He called me to fight against the enemy. I got caught up in names and opinions; until, like Israel, I forgot that all the Lord had to do was stretch out His hand against His enemies. All He did was send me into the battle to represent Him. It is He who will do the fighting. I was caught up in being *the called* and not *the chosen.*

I had abandoned my reality and therefore brought a woe upon myself. Israel thought that by enlisting others for what seemed to be their many *resources*, they abandoned the *Source*—which is *God* Himself. God has the ability to show Himself mighty to save and strong to deliver. All He has to do is stretch forth His hand. If we would seek His kingdom first and His righteousness, all other things will be added onto us.

I had to repent. I was wooed by what appeared to be a show of strength. But my *Woos* quickly turned into *Woes*. Woe, because God is wise, and He knows our ending from our beginning. *We* are dazzled with the show of power. The neighing of the war horses and the glitter of the golden chariot and the flashing steel of the warriors all resembled strength. But God said to Israel, *"This is not your strength. This may succeed for a time, but it is an empire held by the throat, not by the heart."*

That's when I understood life – life is a corkscrew that can't be straightened. I a minus, that won't add up. I said to myself, "I know more and I'm wiser. I've stock-piled wisdom and knowledge." And what I've finally concluded is that so-called wisdom and knowledge are mindless and witless—nothing but spitting in the wind. Much learning earned me much trouble. The more you know, the more you hurt.

From this valuable lesson I've also learned that they who wait upon the Lord shall renew their strength; they shall mount up with wings as eagles; they shall run, and not be weary; and they shall walk and not faint. I've learned that depending on man is like seeking help from an oppressor. But waiting on the Lord is like wait-ing on an inheritance. You know it is coming; it's just that you have to *wait* until its appointed time to be *re-leased* to you.

Israel eventually won the war against the Assyrians. While Hezekiah clad himself in sackcloth out of anguish from the psychological warfare that the Assyrians were raging during the siege, Isaiah assured Hezekiah that the city would be delivered and Sennacherib would be cut down with the sword.

During the night, an angel of the Lord brought death to 185,000 Assyrian troops; and when Sennacherib saw the destruction wreaked on his army, he withdrew to Nineveh. Jerusalem was spared destruction.

Precious hearts, you may be in a psychological warfare of some sort, and may feel that the only way you can defeat the oppressor is by enlisting the help of the oppressors. But I've come, like Isaiah did to Hezekiah while in anguish. You are not going to be destroyed. Just be obedient, pray and let God work out the logistics. *Come out of the corner—I did. Stop crying—I did. Rejoice—I did.*

*Why?* I was looking at the wrong methods *of winning.* You're already a winner, sir, and ma'am. Just look up— help is on the way! If we will draw nigh unto God, He will draw nigh to us. Don't stay there, come on out!

| The Word: |
| :---: |

- Psalm 20:7
- Psalm 40:4
- Psalm 50:10
- Psalm 140:3
- Proverbs 4:33
- Isaiah 26:3
- Isaiah 31:1-3
- Isaiah 60:17
- Jeremiah 17:7-10
- Ecclesiastes 1:15-18
- Matthew 6:33
- Matthew 12:34
- 2 Corinthians 5:7
- James 1:8

- James 4:10
- 1 John 4:18

## The Prayer:

"Father, it is because of Your mercies that I am not consumed. Thank You for delivering me, even in my time of ignorance, and giving me another chance. Thank You for revealing to me that You are the Way, the Truth and the Life; and that it's only in You that I live, that I move and that I have my being. In Jesus' Name, I pray. Amen."

# NOT GUILTY

*"Keep moving ahead and don't look back!"* said the voice behind us. We were moving ever so quickly. It seemed like there were millions of us; however, it was only a few.

As I looked down beneath me, it felt as if I was walking on cobblestoned streets. The pathway was so narrow, I thought that I'd fall out of line. One wrong move and I would have. It was so easy to fall out of place and I knew that if I did, someone was eagerly waiting to take the position in which I once stood.

So I prayed that God would give me the strength to continue to walk the straight and narrow way.

As we walked, we were right behind the other. There really wasn't any room for error. We were so close, that I could feel the breath of the person behind me. Their breaths were short and determined. I finally decided that I was going to speak up, to encourage everyone who was on the line to move ahead. I didn't know why I had the idea to do so, or who I thought I was to take it upon myself to make such an announcement. What authority did *I* possess?

I was in the same predicament as those in front of me and those behind me. *Yet,* "No soul left behind, stay focused, be encouraged, we're almost there," came the

181

words out of my mouth. Soon the multiple voices of men, women and children—all in agreement—responded, *"Amen."*

We walked and we walked. The road seemed like an eternity. As I looked ahead, I could see nothing. I could hear but I couldn't see. We sounded like an army of people, a sea of individuals on their way to who-knows-where. I asked the person in front of me, *"Excuse me, ma'am, do you know where we're going? Do you know where this road leads?"*

She kept walking at first to ignore me, but she wasn't actually ignoring me at all. It was as if her eyes were fixed. As she marched forward, she stated in a tone that was just above a whisper, and with a smile in her voice, *"My friend, we're on our way to the Kingdom to see the King!"*

With those simple words, I tried to make sense of what she was talking about. What did she mean, *we were on our way to the Kingdom to see the King? What kingdom? What King?* I thought. As we continued walking, I heard that voice again. *"Keep moving ahead and don't look back!"* It warned, but the more the voice spoke, the more I was *tempted* to look back.

Just when temptation started to get the best of me, I looked to my right and saw a really large rock. But, upon further scrutiny, I realized it wasn't a rock at all, but it was a pillar of salt. My mind immediately went to the scriptures in Genesis when God delivered Lot and his family out of Sodom and Gomorrah. He warned them not to look back. As they were making their way to safety, Lot's wife look back and turned into a pillar of salt.

At that moment, chills ran down my spine. That could have easily been me. I was so fascinated by that pillar of salt that I, too, almost looked back. By this time, I almost fell out of line. I thought about all the times the Lord brought me out of something—how He delivered me from something I had gotten myself into. Many times God sent help and warnings. Many times I ignored those warnings, thinking I knew what was best. I was thanking God now. Had I stayed in those places *out of which* God was trying to deliver me, and *from* the people he was trying to deliver me, I would've turned bitter—*like salt*—like *Lot's wife.*

As we continued on our journey, I was wondering why it was taking so long to get to the Kingdom. If felt as if I was in a traffic jam. While on line, I tried to start conversations with those in front of and behind me, but to no avail. While thinking, I heard a hideous scream and I almost looked back. But then the warning came to us again, *"Keep moving ahead and don't look back!"* Word had reached me, words that I was to pass along to encourage those before me: Someone had gotten out of line and fell. They were so close, but yet so far. They had looked back.

As the processional continued, we all began to sing. The amazing thing about it was we all sounded harmoniously perfect. As we sang in harmony, it dawned on me that this was the first time I was hearing the song. How was I able to sing a song so perfectly, yet I never heard it before? Even though the song to my recollection had never been sung, the words to the song were familiar to me. We just sang different variations of *"Hallelujah!"*

As we marched ahead, I noticed that we were moving swiftly. As we walked up those cobblestones, I looked down and saw blood. I had noticed these crimson stains all along, but never noticed it in this much detail. Who had come before us, and whose blood was this? These were some of the questions in my head. Had someone gotten hurt ahead of us? As far as I could see, no one had fallen out of line; those ahead of me were determined to make it to the end.

As the journey continued, I grew weary. I felt faint. As if he could read my mind, the male voice behind me said, *"Don't do it! Don't give up, you've come too far."* I then noticed a hand taking me under the arm and encouraging me. He said to me, *"You will reap a harvest of blessings if you faint not!"*

Right then and there, I thought about all the people who had started out with me but hadn't continued. They started on the journey, but for some reason or another walked away, without a trace, without a cause. Some went back to the places where they started, and settled for what was. They didn't have faith enough to continue forward, while others blamed someone else for why they couldn't continue.

I'd sometimes hear their reasoning: *"They wouldn't let me,"* or *"They told me no,"* or *"She said I can't"* or *"My pastor told me this wasn't my time."* All I could do is remember again in the scriptures, "You did run well but who hindered you?"

I started to thank the guy for helping me to stay focused. I must admit that I was losing balance, and I was grateful that this stranger helped me stay on course. As I spoke up to thank him, a woman replied, "It's too late, while helping you, he himself has fallen!" Just that quickly, without a sound, without as much as a whimper, he was gone.

At this point it was dangerous. The road had grown so narrow, it felt as I were on a tightrope. One wrong move and I would tumble into the never-ending darkness below me. A darkness that haunted me. A darkness that I knew was oh, so ready to consume me. I was afraid, but I was also determined. I spoke to my fears through faith, and reminded myself that I can do all things through Christ who strengthens me. If I hadn't needed the Lord at any other time, I surely did need Him now.

We walked through a maze of detours, where many were lost along the way. We walked through mountains and valleys, low places and high places, cold places and desert wind. Although there were others around me, most times I felt so alone. At that moment I knew I had to work out my own salvation with fear and trembling. I was too close to my journey's end and I wouldn't trade it for anything in the world.

There, right before us, I saw a door. The door was huge and looked like it was from medieval times. The door had bars with one humongous lock. Right in the middle of the door was a slot. As we moved toward the door, I noticed something that caused fear to engulf my whole being. When the people stood before the door and knocked, someone looked through the slot and asked them their names.

One by one after announcing their names, they were let in and immediately the door was locked before the next person could go through it. Out of nowhere there was screaming and sobbing at the door. Someone had made it all the way to the door but their name wasn't written in the book! They cried, *"You have to let me in, you just have to let me in!"* *"He knows me, ask Him, He'll tell you!"* They cried, but to no avail.

Suddenly the door slot opened and the voice behind the door said, *"You are fraudulent and of a stolen identity.* *"All of your life you have emulated others!"* *"You had selfish ambitions and your whole goal in the kingdom was to surpass others. You imitated others and you did this with absolute jealousy and rivalry.*

"You stole God's credit and used His name to your own advantage. You told people the Almighty said things that He did not give you—the authority to speak!"

You called yourself an Apostle; God didn't! You called yourself a Prophet; Yahweh didn't! You called yourself an Evangelist, but where are your works? Whom did you evangelize? A pastor you claimed to be and many have strayed because of you. A teacher you weren't because you refused instruction. The blind leading the blind, you have all fallen into the ditch! Many have turned away from Jehovah God because of you, and you will not enter in!"

Just like that, the sobbing individual was gone, engulfed in the darkness below. Suddenly it was my turn. I stood at that enormous door, shaking like a reed in the wind. My hand involuntarily knocked, the slot was opened and my lips voluntarily gave my name. The door was opened. I was relieved, there were many things that could've qualified me a place in the outer darkness.

As I made my way through the gate, I heard the voice say, *"Keep moving and don't look back! You've made it through the gate, but you haven't made it to the kingdom yet. Remember the righteous will barely make it in!"*

I kept on going, and as I was walking, I thought the road would widen. But it didn't; it was still narrow and straight. I looked to my left and I saw what appeared to be a sea of people who were all going in the opposite direction. I tried calling out to them and it was to no avail. Suddenly, there in the midst of the people, I began to see faces—faces I recognized, faces of the people I had known in another time...in another life.

In the sea of people whom I recognized were government officials, church leaders, co-workers, family, friends, and ex-lovers alike. As I looked at them I could almost remember them and the time we spent together. There was something about my mind which now couldn't quite recall the specifics of the events. I felt renewed somehow. I could see their secret sins and I was shocked! I saw the sins of adultery and fornication, sins of uncleanness and lasciviousness.

I was amazed by the amount of idolatry and witchcraft, hatred and variance, emulations and wrath. There was much strife and sedition, heresy and untold amounts of envying. There were those who murdered others verbally and physically. There were all kinds of reveling. My God, have mercy! That once was me. All of them at one point and time were me!

Wait a minute, that could have been me on the other side, I thought. These people are on their way to...*hell?*

*That's it! I'm on my way to the Kingdom to see the King! But why aren't they coming with me?* I began to scream out, "Hey, Hey! You're going the wrong way!" Some of the names that I could remember, I called, but they couldn't hear me.

It was too late. A voice of what I now know to be an angel said, *"The Almighty has spoken and their judgment set. He warned them many times, but they were blinded by the god of the earth. They would rather believe a lie than the truth. They operated in the workings of their flesh and now are on their way to their reward."*

Right there on the path, I asked the angel, where are we? He said to me, *"You're on the Highway called Holiness. Do not weep for those whom Yahweh has rejected. Wipe your eyes and move forward."*

*"Keep moving ahead and don't look back! You've made it through the gate, but you haven't made it to the Kingdom yet! Remember, the righteous shall barely make it in!"*

It was too late. The judgment was set, and there was no more warning to give.

The fear that gripped my heart was untold. If I had to do it all over again, I'd be faithful to God. I'd love more. Something inside of me dreaded going any closer. I knew that this day would come. But was I *ready* for it?

I sat in church Sunday after Sunday, hearing the same message about the return of the Lord Jesus Christ and to be prepared. During the altar call, the choir would sing *"Is Your All on the Altar?"* I wept every single time because, in some way, I knew that I had failed God and humanity. I feverishly laid myself at the altar and asked God to deliver me from hurt and bitterness. I would ask Him to forgive me, because I had, at one point in time, let life consume me.

One Sunday at the *altar,* God *altered* me. I could feel the change in my heart. At that moment, I truly began to love people I knew hated me. I was more honest and, even if I had the slightest thought of doing wrong, I prayed for forgiveness.

I knew a long time ago whether you're a churchgoer or not, when death came, it was so bold that it'll walk right in the church, past everyone else's pew, tap you on the shoulder and say, *"Let's go!"*

I'd seen someone die right in the church. While everyone was shouting and dancing, I was wondering what would become of that person's soul.

I kept on walking and I knew that time for me had run out. I knew that this ultimately was the day. There would be no turning back for me. No more chances, no more messages, no more prayers or Scriptures to quote. I thought about all of my friends and family I'd left behind, and all of those who had gone before. If they had to walk this same road, I was afraid that many of them I wouldn't see again. I know the preacher said, as they closed those caskets for the final time, that we'd see them on the other side. Now, I wasn't so sure about *that*.

I finally made it! I stood there at the judgment! I'd made it all the way to the door. With all that I had witnessed, any ounce of self-righteousness I had quickly dissipated. The only thing I could stand on now was faith and grace. I'd seen so much and witnessed so little. Those who I thought were going to be there weren't; and those who I thought didn't stand a chance, were there.

I wasn't quite home free yet. Yes, my name had been called, but I had to make it in. When my name was called, there was a list a mile long that had everything that I had ever said or done written on it. Whether idle or not, there it was. My earthly mind certainly didn't remember half of those things I had done. My spirit man wept because he knew. *I was guilty.*

I was so ashamed and there was nowhere for me to hide. I knew that this was the day that I would have to give an account of my life. The Lord stood there, shining brighter than the sun—a glory that could not be compared. The glory was so bright that it exposed all I thought I could hide and all that I thought I could wash away. That's when the Lord spoke from His throne. He said to me, *"Remember when you were on those cobblestoned streets?"*

He said, "They represented life and how rough it could be. Those cobblestones represented how easy it was to trip and fall when you weren't focused, and how you could easily look back and make a detour for something more convenient, a smoother pathway.

"However, you noticed something on the pathway that many others didn't. You noticed *the blood!* You noticed *My blood,* and when you noticed *My blood,* you didn't understand why you were where you were, or how you'd gotten there. All you knew was that if you just followed *the blood, that the blood would lead you to safety!"* He said, *"I know you, I love you. I gave my life to save you. Love paid the price for mercy. Your verdict—Not guilty!*

*"Well done, you good and faithful servant. You have been faithful over a few things. I will make you ruler over many things. Enter now into the joy of the Lord."*

| The Word: |
|---|

- Matthew 15:8
- Matthew 17:13-14
- Matthew 25:21
- Isaiah 35:8
- Ephesians 4:11
- Luke 9:26

- Galatians 5:7,19-21
- Galatians 6:9
- 1 Peter 3:8-10
- 1 Peter 4:18-19
- Nehemiah 8:1-3
- Philippians 2:15
- Philippians 4:13
- Genesis 19:26
- 1 Corinthians 9:27
- Psalms 23:4
- Romans 1:25
- 1 Samuel 15:10-11
- 2 Thessalonians 2:11

## The Prayer:

"Heavenly Father, have mercy on me, a sinner. I believe in You and that Your Word is true. I believe that Jesus Christ is the Son of the Living God and that He died on the cross that I may have forgiveness for my sins and eternal life.

I believe in my heart that You, Lord God, raised Him from the dead. Please, Jesus, forgive me for every sin I have ever committed or done in my heart. I give You my life for the rest of my life. I ask that You take full control from this moment on. I pray this in the Name of Jesus Christ. Amen."

# HIS TESTIMONY
# FROM HER LIPS


*"Marlene, honey, it's time to get going. The limousines will be here to pick us up any minute,"* Eugene said softly to his wife.

*"Give me a minute, Gene, I'll be down shortly,"* she replied. Marlene looked around the room one more time, tracing every piece of furniture with her index finger.

She looked around the room and admired the many trophies and medals that lined the walls. She looked up at the smiling face with the pearly white teeth. She smiled, remembering how Gene would wake up their son Jules every morning as a child, and take him into the bathroom to show him how to brush his teeth. She remembered Gene shaving, how Gene sprayed some of the shaving crème into Jules' little hands and watched how Jules imitated his father.

She laughed, remembering how Jules' little fingers used the plastic knife Gene had given him and how he pretended it was a razor. He'd say, *"See, daddy, look, I'm shaving too!"*

Gene nicked himself shaving and began to bleed. Jules said, *"Daddy, look, you have a boo-boo."* Jules climbed down off the wooden stepstool and got Gene a washcloth. He walked back into the bathroom and placed the washcloth under the cold water and said firmly, *"Look, dad, this may sting a little bit, but try not to cry. You're a big boy, okay?"*

Gene, holding in his laughter, looked at his son and said, *"Sure, I'll try not to cry."* Jules took the cloth and wiped away the small amount of blood. He said, *"See, daddy, you're a champ. Now hurry up, my school bus will be here and I need you to show me how to tie my shoes again."*

Marlene stood in that room and cried. All she and Gene would have of Jules now would be pictures and fading memories. Why? She cried. *Why did it have to happen to my son?* Sobbing, she felt a soft touch on her shoulder.

She looked around, believing it to be Gene, but there was no one there. She looked over and saw that the window was slightly ajar, so she chalked it up to the wind.

Moments later, she looked out the window and saw the limousines pull up. She noticed her mother and sister standing in front of her home, holding hands and consoling each other. She noticed the funeral director coming out of the limousine, talking to Gene. She knew it was time to make her way down the steps.

Just last week she stood in the same doorway as she and Gene waved goodbye to Jules who, with his girlfriend Sarah, had just gotten into the limousine and were on their way to their senior prom. Marlene stood there in his room now, wishing that her *goodbye* that night wasn't her *final goodbye.* Who would have ever thought she really would be saying goodbye for the final time? Had she known, she reasoned within herself, she wouldn't have let him go. But reality was, he still would've gone.

She noticed in the last couple of months that Jules was acting a bit erratic. She and Gene had chalked it down to nerves and growing pains. Jules had said some hurtful things to both her and Gene. But they decided that they wouldn't let it harden their hearts. He was their son; and of course he didn't really mean what he said at times.

Many days in the Dixon home, arguments were ignited. Whenever Jules was asked to do something he didn't want to do—like clean up his room or go to church— he would protest. Sometimes those protests would turn ugly. Jules would break things or use profanity, which Gene would automatically correct.

But most times the night would end with an *"I'm sorry"* from Jules. Because they were loving, caring, kind-hearted Christian parents, Gene and Marlene always hugged him and told him it was all right. They called him by his childhood nickname, *"Nugget,"* the one his grandparents had given him as a baby.

Jules knew that whenever his mom or dad called him *"Nugget,"* he'd won them over and all was forgiven.

Jules started dating Sarah in their sophomore year at Christ Is King Christian Academy. When they first started dating, he was head-over-heels in love with Sarah.

Marlene had found herself jealous, as any mother would. Some other woman, even though Sarah was far from being a woman, had taken an interest in her one and only son. Marlene knew this day would eventually come. Still, in her heart of hearts, she wasn't prepared to let her "Nugget" leave the nest.

But if he was determined to be with Sarah, she would make sure that Sarah didn't break his heart. She was confident in knowing that Gene had done such a fine job raising Jules, and that her baby would be a perfect gentleman to Sarah.

However, there was something about Sarah that really bothered Marlene. Marlene didn't quite know how to feel about this young girl who was stealing her son's heart. When Marlene looked at Sarah, she didn't recognize herself.

She knew that most men dated women who had some kind of trace of their mother; but in Sarah, she saw none. She even heard that Sarah had a reputation over at the Academy for being such a loose girl. Marlene hoped that Jules hadn't done anything sexual with Sarah.

Though Gene and Jules had a confidentiality agreement between father and son, Gene still secretly told Sarah almost everything that Jules had confided in him. Up to the point of his death, she knew that her son still hadn't had any sexual relations with Sarah or any other girl.

She wouldn't have imagined in a million years that her

son Jules was doing drugs, though. That explained the erratic behavior and emotional outburst. Marlene and Gene found out a few days after the accident that Sarah had introduced Jules to heroin.

When Jules and Sarah got into the accident the night of their prom, it was said they were getting high on their way back. The limousine driver said that he smelled something unusual. He rolled down the window and saw that the kids were getting high.

The driver said that he asked them to put out the drugs or he'd have to put them out and report them to the police. That's when one of the classmates started to yell and scream at him.

According to the police statement, when the limousine driver went to pull over, he was struck in the head with a liquor bottle that one of the teens had brought into the limousine. The driver immediately lost consciousness and the limousine flipped over. Almost everyone in the limousine died—everyone except for Sarah, the limo driver and the young man who hit the driver in the back of his head.

Jules, however, had been thrown from the limousine. They said he was so high, he probably died *before* landing in the fields ahead.

Marlene closed the door behind her and made her way to the top of the stairs landing. When she got there, Gene was at the bottom of the stairs looking up at her. He could see that, within a week, his beloved had aged significantly.

There was nothing he could do to console her. He knew, now that Jules was gone, their lives would never be the same. They thought, not only were they going to say goodbye to the body, but also to his *soul.*

Everything in Marlene was mad at God. *"You took my son,"* she said over and over that week. She was bitterly angry with the Lord. She soon realized that she had not done the best she could by Jules. She and Gene had given them all that he could ever ask for. When Jules didn't want to go to church, she and Gene said it was fine; that he could stay home and play games or watch sports, or go to hang out with friends. Now, she regretted it.

What really plagued her was she never witnessed her son giving his life to the Lord. Yes, he had gotten christened as a baby and yes, he was baptized as a child. But she never saw him publicly confess Jesus as his personal Lord and Savior. Though he was a member of the church, he didn't serve in any capacity. Jules had only gone to church because his mother and father asked him to. She had come to pray that somewhere, somehow, Jules had accepted Christ as his own personal Lord and Savior; that he had somehow, someway repented of his sins. She would never know for sure.

As they made their way to the church, she and Gene just held on to each other. They kept their eyes closed the whole time as if they were lost in a deep dream. Once the car stopped, they would wake up. When the limousine pulled up in front of the church, the driver got out and opened the door. Marlene's parents and sister got out first, followed by Gene's mother and older brother. It was now time for Gene and Marlene to step out of the car. With all those people standing there waiting and looking, Marlene couldn't muster up the strength to move.

Gene looked over at the woman he loved and married, and delicately helped her out of the car. She took one step out and she began to sob. You could hear gasps and wails from those standing around. Gene took her by one hand and her mother took her by the other. Slowly they made their way into the church, down the aisle, this time to say *goodbye*.

Sitting in the funeral services for Jules Jermaine Dixon, Marlene was overtaken with grief. She just sat there in a daze. Many portions of the service had already taken place, and from one face to the next, they all looked the same—blurry. She was resting her head on Gene's shoulder as the soloist had just finished a rendition of "Precious Lord," when the funeral suddenly went abuzz!

Gene looked back to see what all the fuss was about. When he turned back around, the concern in his eyes made Marlene get up to see for herself where all of the whispering and murmurs were coming from. Before she could turn all the way around, Gene warned her to just rest her head on his shoulder and stay focused. But she couldn't. She *had* to see what all of the ruckus was about. She noticed through swollen eyes and a tear-stained face—Sarah being wheeled down the aisle by some of her and Jules' fellow classmates.

Everything in Marlene wanted to scream at her, snatch one of the crutches out of her hand and beat her with it. She wanted to curse and scream, "What are you doing here?" but she couldn't. Every time she went to open her mouth, her lips shook. She couldn't form the words her heart wanted to say, even in her grief. Looking at Sarah made her heart ache; for the girl—the girl who should have, in her heart of hearts, died instead of her Jules.

Marlene quickly repented of her thoughts. She wouldn't wish this pain, this sorrow, this anguish on any other parent, not even Sarah's.

When the mourners calmed themselves, Sarah rolled herself toward the microphone. *What would she say? How dare she?* were the questions on everyone's mind. With the aid of one of the young men from their school, she was handed the microphone. In tears, Sarah looked around the sanctuary, and could feel the judgment and rage coming from everyone in attendance. However, there was something she needed to say, even in the face of all those who resented her at the moment.

Sarah opened her mouth and she spoke:

*"Today, I know many of you are wondering why is she here? I know some of you, if not all of you, must be saying to yourself, she has a lot of nerve wheeling herself in here, much less getting the microphone to speak."*

A few harsh '*Amen's* rang throughout the church.

*"I'm here today to celebrate the life of not only my friend, but the love of my life, Jules. 'J.J.', as I called him, was very patient with me. As you know, we both attended Christ Is King Christian Academy. What many of you didn't know was that Jules met me when my life was at its lowest point.*

*"I am a pastor's child and my parents are here with me today. You see, I couldn't cope with all the attention that came with being a P.K. That's what we call ourselves, P.K.—preacher's kid. So I started to hang out with some of the neighboring kids and that led to some peer pressure. By my own volition, I chose to participate in some drug use.*

*"I know rumor has it that Jules was on drugs because I introduced him to it. But I want to set the record straight. He was not. Not only did I not introduce him to drugs, he wasn't on any. He was secretly taking me to rehab every weekend. I would meet up with him and we'd go to see my drug counselor. We bumped into some of our classmates coming out of the treatment facility, and before I could come clean, J.J. took the slack and said that we were there for him. He loved me, he covered me!"* she cried.

*"J.J. became irritated with me at times because he was so stressed. He told me that his parents thought he was on drugs. He also confided in me that any little thing he was asked to do caused tension in their home because of me. He could be a bit short-tempered,"* she laughed.

"*Excuse me for laughing,*" Sarah said. "*Jules was such a sweetheart. I couldn't imagine him being short-tempered with anyone. But we all know.*" The mourners smiled and laughed along.

"*Jules started a prayer and bible study at Christ Is King. It's funny, we went to a Christian Academy but rarely did Christian activities. He started the prayer group and often times would lead us into prayer every morning. That's how we started our days—in prayer—and then a short bible study during lunch. I asked Jules why he stopped going with his parents to church. He told me he no longer went because he couldn't relate to the preaching: there was nothing at the church targeted for the younger generation. He said that everything was programmed with little change—more religion than relationship. As he studied his bible, he noticed that the preaching was more theatrical than truthful.*

"*He wanted more teaching than just hearing somebody whoop and walk across chairs. He always laughed and said the only time the congregation moved is when the musicians started playing the organ while the pastor was preaching. By then, all was lost. He could no longer understand or hear what the preacher was saying, other than the occasional 'I can't hear nobody' or the 'say yes!' Or the famous 'Hey glory' the preacher threw in every other word.*

"*Once we had a guest theologian come to the Academy, and I saw*"—she paused— "*Jules walk up to the stage with tears streaming down his face, repenting as he accepted Jesus as his personal Lord and Savior.*"

Marlene let out a scream.

*"He told me,"* Sarah continued in tears, *"that he went home that night and apologized to his parents; and his mother, who calls him 'Nugget,' and his father both forgave him. I always told him that we were blessed to have the loving parents we have. The night of the prom, when we were on our way back home, one of our classmates pulled out some heroin and asked us if we wanted to join in on the party. Jules told him, 'No.'*

*"I began to shake uncontrollably, because temptation was right in my face, and though I thought I was over drugs, I guess I really didn't know until I was tested. When Ty started to prepare the drugs, Jules knocked on the glass to get the driver's attention to pull over, but the music was too loud and he couldn't hear him knocking. Ty had, at this point, begun to cook the heroin in a spoon and that's when the driver rolled down the window. He told us either put it out or he'd put us out and call the police. But Jules and I explained to him that we weren't doing it. Ty and his date were.*

*"Ty started screaming something about the police. That's when he went on the inside of his tuxedo jacket, pulled out a liquor bottle and struck the driver in the back of the head. The car exhilarated and the next thing I knew, were in the air,"* she recalled, sobbing.

*"The last thing I remember is waking up in the hospital, reaching for Jules, and he wasn't there.*

*"Mr. and Mrs. Dixon, I want you to know that the Jules you raised and the Jules you saw on his way to the prom last week is the same Jules. Because of him, many are saved and living for Christ. It was he who told us that we needed a relationship with the Lord Jesus Christ and that we needed Jesus to be our Savior. You see, yes, I'm a P.K. I went to church because I had no choice. After experiencing J.J., I experienced Jesus. I started going back to church this time because of choice—my choice now was to serve Christ.*

*"Know that his living wasn't in vain. Know that he couldn't be pressured into anything. Know that his response to peer pressure was, 'my parents would kill me.' Like the gold bracelet we wore, WWJD, he'd say, 'What Would Jesus Do?'"*

The congregation who once sat in judgment and anger now rose to their feet in praise. Their hearts were changed toward the young woman who now stood before them free of their judgments and opinions. She had gotten up and spoke well and truthfully about the young man she'd always carry in her heart. She knew that morning that she would be taking a risk going to the services, but something in her told her she needed to go.

Before she left her house, she felt as if someone had touched her on the shoulder. When she looked around she noticed that one of the windows was left ajar, and she chalked it up to having been a small breeze.

The preacher at this point didn't say a word. He knew that the eulogy had been given. All he needed to do was to stand and extend an invitation to salvation through Christ.

He looked out toward the masses of people who stood in the church; and in his heart he pondered a way to change his preaching style to an effective *reaching* style. Without a whoop, a holler, a say yes or walking on a chair, he said these words, *"Beloved of the Lord, the bible says that the Word, God's Message in Christ, is near you, on your lips and in your heart. That is the Word, the message, the basis and object of faith of which we preach.*

*"Precious hearts, the Word of the Lord says to us, if you would just acknowledge and confess with your lips that Jesus is Lord; and in your heart believe, adhere to, trust in, and rely on the truth that God raised Him from the dead, guess what, beloved? You will be saved.*

*"For with the heart a person believes, we adhere to, trust in, and rely on Christ and so is justified. We're declared righteous, acceptable to God; and with the mouth confess. I have no gimmicks. Come declare openly and speak out freely your belief in Jesus as your Lord and personal Savior, and this will confirm your salvation.*

*"The scriptures say, "No man who believes in Christ will ever be put to shame or be disappointed, no one. For in Christ there is no distinction between Jew and Greek. The same Lord is Lord over all of us, and He generously bestows His riches upon all who call upon Him in faith.*

*For everyone who calls upon the Name of Jesus as their Lord and Savior will be saved ...will you come?"*

At this point Marlene had risen from her seat. With tears still flowing down her face, she walked over to Sarah, and hugged her. Marlene hugged her as if she were hugging her own child. The Lord had answered Marlene's prayer. She knew her "Nugget" was saved and loved the Lord. Her son had been eulogized. Though the pain and grief would never go away and her family's life would never be the same, Marlene found comfort in knowing that *her son* introduced *the Son*, and *through salvation*, today many will be redeemed.

Sometimes through the loss of a loved one, God will get the glory. From the beginning of time, parents have had to bury their babies, starting with Adam and Eve in the Garden – to Mary when she watched her son Jesus Christ as he lay crucified on the cross for the sins of the world.

Mother, father, if you're reading this and have lost a child, you're not alone – you're *not* alone. Jesus knows, He cares and He will comfort you. Sometimes we don't understand God's will or His plans, but we must trust Him, knowing that He doesn't make mistakes, but that His mercy endures forever and will get us through anything.

| The Word: |
| --- |

- Genesis 4:8-11
- Genesis 9:6

- Exodus 21:12
- Matthew 5:16
- Matthew 18:15
- John 3:16-18
- Romans 10:8-13,
- Romans 12:19
- Romans 13:1-14
- Galatians 6:1-10
- Philippians 3:10
- 1 John 3:16
- 1 Kings 3:19
- 2 Kings 4
- Mark 5:21-43
- Proverbs 22:6
- Proverbs 127:3
- 1 Samuel 1:20
- 2 Corinthians 4:16-18
- 1 Thessalonians 4:13-17

## The Prayer:

"Father, it is Your will that none should perish, but that all should come to repentance. Today I pray that I may know You and the power of Your resurrection, and the fellowship of Your sufferings.

Thank You for the grace to know You more. Thank You that You held me together until I got it together, that all

I've done or will ever do has already been nailed to the cross. Thank You, because whatever the enemy thinks he has over my head is already under Your feet.

Thank You for the efficacious blood of Jesus. I AM HEALED, because of the blood. In Jesus' Name, I pray and count it all done. Amen."

# THE STRUGGLE IS OVER

The struggle is over. Yes, you! I'm talking to you! Your struggles are over and guess what: You may be broken and you may even have been bruised. You may even have a few battle scars to show that you've been in a fight. But that's good. You need to have something to show the enemy that you are not where they left you.

Gladly get up and receive your crown of righteousness. Receive your reward for enduring to the end. I'm so glad you made it. I was in heaven watching as you made your way to the finish line. I was cheering you on further from the balconies of glory. I told the devil, "you won't win this one—this one here is a winner!"

We were excited about your race. We saw you get tired and we saw the determination in you to go all the way. You were just running and running. No matter what obstacles came your way, you leapt over them like you had hind feet. You took a tumble here and there. But you never let those minor mishaps keep you from the bigger picture.

We saw when you received those rejection letters, when you cried because you felt that by now you should have made it all the way through. Then, instead of looking at rejection as a defeat, you looked at it as victory.

You began to see what it is God wanted you to see all

along, that when people *reject* you, they are really *validating* you. You understood that rejection was someone's way of saying that you really *have* what it takes to make it. They just didn't want to encourage you in the thing you were set to accomplish. Because, if they did, you'd outdo them.

They didn't see that what you did wasn't based on competition. It was based on *love*. You loved people. You knew that what was in you could be a blessing to so many others, had you the opportunity—just one opportunity. You waited and you waited; and you cried many tears. Hurt and pain become your comfort at one point. But here in heaven, we kept cheering you on.

*You can do it! You can make it,* cried the voices of those of us who went before you. Yeah, you cried. What great man or woman doesn't cry? What warrior doesn't weep? Sometimes wailing is a sign of war. It was good that you were afflicted, because you learned. You cried so much so, until your tears washed away that hurt and pain.

Look over there and tell me, what do you see? Yeah—you see that man. That man's name was Stephen. You see, darling, whenever you're chosen by God to bring change, you'd better be ready to go through some pain—I mean some *real pain*. You see those smiling faces—they have stones behind their backs! People don't mind using you as long as you don't mess with their apple cart.

In the book of Acts, as the word of God prospered and the disciples were increasing in numbers by leaps and bounds, the Greeks had begun to have hard feelings against the Hebrews because their widows were being discriminated against in the food lines.

So the twelve disciples called a meeting and thought that it wouldn't be right to abandon their responsibilities of preaching and teaching the word of God to help with the care of the poor. So they had the people choose seven men whom everyone trusted. These were men of the Holy Spirit and good sense, so that they could be assigned the task by the disciples of handling this discrimination, and so that the disciples could continue their work without interruption.

The congregation thought it was a *marvelous* idea. They chose Stephen, a man full of faith and the Holy Spirit; Philip, Procorus, Nicanor, Timon, Parmenas and Nicolas, a convert from Antioch. God's word prospered, and discipleship grew. Stephen, *brimming* with God's unmerited favors and unsurpassed energy, was doing great things among the people so much so, that it was unmistakable that God was among them.

Some men now went up against Stephen and argued with him. However, they were no match for his wisdom and spirit when he spoke. So in secret they bribed men to lie. These lied and said that they heard Stephen cursing Moses and God. The people were stirred up; and the religious leaders and scholars of the religious order grabbed Stephen and took him before the High Council.

There the liars came forth, saying that not only was Stephen talking against the Holy Place and God's law; they said they heard him say that Jesus of Nazareth would tear the place down and throw out all the customs Moses had given them. All the people who were on the High Council looked at Stephen, unable to take their eyes off of him. His face was like the face of an angel!

So, you've cried because you've been lied on. *Boo-hoo, poor you.* You thought that because you were full of wisdom and truth, and because you have the Spirit of the Lord dwelling on the inside of you, that everyone would just love you—especially those with whom you fellowship, and those who work with you in ministry.

No, on the contrary, it made you a target. Yes, you were set up. As long as you are appeasing those who sit on the High Council—you know, those people who sit in lofty places and make all the rules for the organization, and God forbid if you question or don't agree with one, or even slightly voice your opinion. Like Alice in Wonderland, it would be *off with your head!* Yeah—that kind of High Council.

What I marvel at in that whole scenario is Stephen had faith and the Holy Spirit. He had wisdom and the ability to produce results. But the people who were on the *"High Council,"* though they could *see* the Spirit of the Lord on Stephen, and were even captivated by him, they still believed the *liars!*

Even when Stephen pleaded his case, they still stoned him to death, to the point where he prayed and asked the Lord to take his life. Yes, we heard you pray that same prayer as you were being stoned by those whom you served, too.

Aren't you glad God doesn't answer every prayer that way?

Standing on the sidelines watching Stephen's murder was Saul, a murderer of the Christians. He would soon become the very thing he tried to kill! So sad people tried to kill you because they thought that, by killing you, they could change God's mind!

Oh, I'm sorry, you still haven't gotten it. Okay, slow learner, I see, it's okay; I may not be patient but God is. Aw, don't feel insulted. Come on, buddy. Maybe this story will cheer you up. Everyone isn't Saul; and everyone isn't a liar. Some of those trials you went through, the Lord purposely had you endure so that He could get the glory out of your life. Enough with that, listen to this story. It's a true story indeed.

There was in the Bible a man named Daniel. He was a prophet and an interpreter of dreams. He was an official in the Persian Empire under the kingship of King Darius. He was also a praying man. A man brought into captivity from his homeland of Judah. The king changed Daniel's name to Belshazzar.

However, Daniel kept the customs and the laws of his people. He refused to defile himself with the royal rations of food and wine. So Daniel asked the palace master not to let him defile himself. God gave Daniel favor and compassion. Though the palace master was afraid of what the king would say and do, he made a deal with Daniel and the other Hebrew Boys anyway; and they were able to grow strong with the help of the Lord.

God gave Daniel favor because of the bigger picture! After escaping the fiery furnace of the prideful King Nebuchadnezzar, Daniel finds himself in crisis again, this time with King Darius. Guess what—you got it. God showed up again! Darius, excuse me—*King Darius*—appointed 120 satraps over the kingdom; and over them, three commissioners, of which Daniel was one. But Daniel, brimming—there goes that word again—with spirit and intelligence, outshone the rest of them. Therefore, the King decided to put Daniel in charge of the *whole* kingdom.

So the satraps, better known as the governors, and the other two vice-regents got together to find some kind of scandal or skeleton in Daniel's closet that they could use—and *bam—Nothing!* So they then conspired together, went to the king and buttered him up as the church folks to the pastor and leaders. With flattery, they said, *"King Darius, live forever!"*

These brown-nosers went on to say to the king that *they* convened and *they* had agreed that the king should issue a decree saying that for the next thirty days, no one was to pray to any god or mortal except to the king. If *anyone* disobeyed, he or she should be thrown into the lions' den.

Not only did they want the king to make the decree, they wanted the king to make it unconditionally, as if written in stone like all the laws of the Medes and the Persians. The king, full of himself as many are, issued the decree—not knowing the motive behind the gathering of the governors, the decree or the outcome.

They figured, if we can't find dirt on Daniel other than the fact that he prays, then we'll make a religious decree that'll cause him to falter. We don't mind him praying— he can pray all he wants. But let's see how faithful to prayer he'll be if we tell him he can no longer pray to *his* King—only to ours.

How many times were you caught up in a scandal because your closet was clean? Now we know *your* name isn't Daniel and you may have some skeletons in your closet. But the good thing is, God's already been in your closet. While you were praying, He went in your closet, removed your skeletons and buried their bones. When your enemies go in there and try to use them against you, the evidence would have been removed.

Daniel heard about the decree and kept praying to God as he always did. Three times a day, with his window wide open toward Jerusalem, he prayed and thanked God, all the while the brown-nosers were listening in and heard Daniel asking God for help.

*They* went straight to the king and reminded *him* of *his* royal decree—the one *he* signed—and reminded him of what he said, and the outcome of what the offender would face. Then they put it on him. *"Daniel, your buddy, he ain't listening to the rules, reverend—and we can't have that. Because of the decree you made, we have no other choice but to have Daniel thrown in the lions' den."*

What I like about the story is that the King said to Daniel, *"Because you're so loyal to your God, He's going to get you out of this!"* The king left after Daniel's supposed fate was sealed and he stood up all night fasting and praying. At daybreak, the king got up and hurried to the lion's den, calling out for Daniel. Daniel was there, awake and responding, *"I'm here!"*

Then Darius—oops, *King Darius*—had Daniel removed out of the den. The conspirators and their families were thrown in. Their fate—death before they could even hit the floor!

You endured all of that and were promoted spiritually every time. You didn't have to sleep with anybody, brown-nose anyone or sell your soul to get to the top. You remained faithful. Now, look what the *Lord* has done! When your conspirators come looking for you, shout: "I'm here!" And as you make your exit, don't forget to thank the lions for letting you use them as a pillow for your head to lay. *God is going to let you rest through your season of persecution.*

## The Word:

- Hebrews 12:1-17
- Acts 6:1-15
- Acts 7:1-60, Acts 8:1
- Daniel 31:1-30, Daniel 6:1-24
- Psalm 71
- Psalm 18:33
- Habakkuk 3:19
- 2 Samuel 22:34

- Psalm 10:2
- 1 Peter 5:8
- Revelation 2:10

> ## The Prayer:

"Father, today I run to You for dear life. Thank You for getting me out of this mess and being a guest room where I can retreat. You said Your door was always open. Thank You for freeing me from the grip of the wicked. Thank You for not watching only from the sidelines.

But You ran to my side and made my accusers lose face. You made them look like idiots. I will daily praise You. All day long I'll chant about You and Your righteous ways, while those who tried to do me in slink off in shame. Thank You for being the help of my countenance. In Jesus' Name. Amen."

# MIRROR, MIRROR
# ON THE WALL

*"Mirror, mirror on the wall, who's the fairest of them all?"*

The mirror answered, *"O, Lady Queen, though fair ye be, there is one fairer far to see..."*

The Queen was horrified, and from that moment on, envy and pride grew in her heart like a rank weed.

When you look at yourself in the mirror, what do you see? Have you ever wished you had the beauty of another?

Have you ever looked at yourself and said, maybe if I had a smaller nose or thinner lips? If only I had a bigger bust or firmer buns. Maybe if I had bigger biceps or larger genitals, they'd love me.

You thought by changing who you are, it would cause others to look at you differently. Maybe if you had hazel eyes instead of blue, you'd be more attractive. But, would that make them *want* you?

Throughout history, we see where men and women have gone through great lengths to change their appearances. Whether it was excessive makeup or a variety of wigs, or an endless collection of designer clothes or shoes – it gave the appearance of having the best, when in reality they had less.

When beauty fades and possessions are lost, you have no other choice but to take a look at who you really are – not who people think you should be. There you are, no makeup, no stylist, no assortment of accessories to doll you up, just you and the mirror.

Now, I ask you the question again. What do you see? Do you see the *real* you, who were made in the image and likeness of God, or do you see a *recreated* you? A recreated you that even *you* don't recognize. You have masqueraded as somebody else for so long, you've lost your identity. Under layers and layers of cosmetics, you don't even remember how your epidermis looked before you covered yourself up.

For years you've been trying to cover your blemishes and flaws. You can't let the world see the *real* you. You can't let them see the real you because they may not *accept* the *real* you. The *real* you may not be as *entertaining*. The *real* you may not be as *funny*. The *real* you just may be the *face* of a clown – the face that brings *laughter* to everyone else, while you yourself sit in the confines of *misery*.

You are no longer the life of the party. When you're home alone and the lights are out and your friends are gone. The voices in your head says, *'Bravo! Bravo! Sing for me, dance for me, and entertain me!'* But you're not an entertainer.

You are a recreated image outside of *purpose* looking into *pain*. You are what everyone else wants you to be. *You* are Pinocchio. You have been carved and sharpened.

Someone has placed strings on you and the only time you can perform is when the puppet master picks you up and says, 'Show time!'

You're a *liar*. Your life has become one lie after another, because you want people to think your fairy tale is real. You want others to believe that you are the master of your own show, when in all actuality, you're absolutely confused and willing to do anything to fit in with everyone. Even if it means to change who you *really* are.

The pride in you refuses to get off the stage, to bow out gracefully. You're like an opera singer past life's prime. You can no longer hit the notes you're loved and adored for. Yet you continue to sell out shows just to appease an audience who painfully watches your light dim, and then walks away feeling cheated, because you are no longer worth the sight to see.

You are imploding and you can't stand it! There's somebody younger, stronger, more beautiful, *so you think*. Therefore, you continue to reinvent yourself. As said in show business, *"The show must go on!"*

What do you see? Tell me, be honest.

Can I tell you what *I* see? I see a person looking into a mirror. A mirror that is broken, but in your eyes, the mirror is whole. Someone dropped the mirror and didn't replace the glass. You'd rather look into a cracked mirror than to replace its glass; because the broken mirror lies to you.

The broken mirror, because it's cracked, can't really show you the crow's feet around your eyes or the laugh frowns that have developed around your mouth. When you look into the cracked mirror, you see a lie, an image of what used to be.

This is the same mirror you used while you covered yourself with the *false* you. This is the same mirror you used to put on costumes of who you *wanted* to be – Can I help you?

The mirror is *broken*. The mirror is just a reflection of who you are. *You*, my dear, *you* are *broken*. You're shattered. Fragmented and sharp, dangerous to the touch.

Covering the mirror won't change anything, but replacing the glass will. You see, you've been living fragmented for far too long. You've been living like a caterpillar for far too long. You think you're so monstrous until all you're good for is to be stepped on.

So daily you dodge the shoes of those who broke your heart. You hide behind the leaves of your past, hoping that you can crawl away out of sight before someone preys on you again.

You crawl up in a ball every time you feel threatened. But crawling up in a ball doesn't protect you, it just exposes the fear transition brings. You see, your mirror's frame isn't the problem, the broken glass is. Broken glass is dangerous; if you don't allow it to be thrown away and replaced, it can cut you and it *will* cause you and everyone else around you to bleed.

The broken glass represents the person who said, '*I love you,*' then stabbed you in your heart. The broken glass represents the smiles that you used to see when your heart believed the empty promises you were being told.

Now, like the caterpillar, you're dodging the inevitable.

Let me help you. I remember being so wounded that I, like you, started to live a lie. My lie protected me. My lie told me that if I made others happy, they'd love me. My *lie* told me that if I changed the way I looked, I would draw the right people. But what my *lie* didn't tell me was, if *I* let my ways please the *Lord, He* would give *me* the *desires* of my *heart.*

You see, I was living in a house filled with cracked mirrors that I had covered. I hid the truth from myself. I became envious and prideful, until one day I uncovered the mirror. I looked at myself and began to speak to *myself* in the mirror. Guess what I started to see?

I started to see myself for what I really was – fearfully and wonderfully made. I saw how ridiculous I looked. My clothes were too small because my pride was too big. The lines that formed around my eyes and mouth were faint, yet graceful. That's when I knew I could transition, and I could change with grace.

I no longer had to perform. I could become the real me, the *new* me. No costume changes, no makeup, no audience, just me. The day I looked into the mirror, I saw the image of God looking back at me. In all my brokenness, I asked, *"Mirror, Mirror, on the wall, who is the fairest of them all?"*

The mirror looked back at me and said, *"O Lady Queen, flawless, you be!"*

I replied, *"Oh, Mirror, what do you mean?"*

The mirror spoke back to me and said, *"When I identify you, I identify you by your flaws, because flaws tells the truth of who you really are. I don't think any less of you, because when I see you, I see me."*

That day, I started my transition. I took down all of the brokenness that surrounded me and replaced it with truth. I knew, if I was going to love the genuine me, I'd have to be processed. It was time that this caterpillar pupates. In order to do that, I had to trust the mirror, I had to now find my truth and weave myself into a chrysalis.

I no longer saw myself as an ugly caterpillar. The more I talked into the mirror, the more I was healed. Once I threw away the shattered pieces and stood in the mirror whole, I got a new concept of what it is to transition gracefully. Those who couldn't accept me for who I was – were no longer welcomed in my heart. God gave me a new image and along with a new image came a *new start*.

He said, let me teach you something about forgiveness. Let me tell you about caterpillars who become butterflies...

*"Your heart was real heavy,*
*Your eyes were filled with tears,*
*How could you make yourself so vulnerable?*
*By sharing your hopes and fears.*

*With the typing of their fingers,*
*And after a series of bliss,*
*Just like that, things changed,*
*And you had quickly been dismissed!*

*Anger mixed with sadness,*
*Disappointment mixed with rage,*
*You wanted to ball up your fist at them,*
*But the Holy Spirit said, 'Behave!'*

*He said, 'Never let the enemy bring you out of character,*
*It's okay, go ahead and cry,*
*This one wasn't meant for you,*
*And here's the reason why...*

*'You were created with a purpose,*
*For someone to share your name.*
*How could they share in your happiness?*
*When they mocked you in your pain.*

*'So I say to you, let the caterpillar crawl on,*
*Go ahead and wipe your eyes,*
*You can't crawl with creeps any longer,*
*Because, you're a butterfly!'"*

*So crawl on, creepy crawler,*
*Remember to dodge the shoes,*
*I trust that you too will become a butterfly,*
*Before someone steps on you!"*

Now I see myself differently. I am fearfully and wonderfully made. I realize that I'm the only one who looks like me.

I have my own DNA. The broken glass has been trashed and the mirror put back in its place. I thank God that He saw me through mercy's eyes and covered me with His grace.

Beloved, know that God loves you as you *are*. No need to hide. Come as you are without pretense. Take off the makeup, let the Lord wash it away. You don't need to cover yourself up with layers of hurt and pain, it will only end with envy and pride. The bible says, *"God delights in His people and He will beautify the meek, [the humble, the plain ole folk] with salvation."*

God wants to give you beauty for ashes, the oil of joy for mourning, the garment of praise for the spirit of heaviness, that you can be called a tree of righteousness, the planting of the Lord that He may be glorified. You are precious in the eyes of God; and the only thing He wants to change about you is your heart.

If He can change your heart, then He can change your mind. He wants to awaken you to the best you. He wants you to see yourself as He sees you - *flawless.*

| The Word: |
|:---:|

- 1 Corinthians 13:12
- 2 Corinthians 4:16
- Proverbs 3:15-18
- Proverbs 31:30
- 1 Peter 3:3-4

- Song of Solomon 4:7
- Psalm 37:4
- Psalm 119:37
- Psalm 139:14
- Psalm 149:4
- Philippians 2:5
- Philippians 4:7-9
- 1 Samuel 16:7
- Jeremiah 4:30
- 1 Timothy 4:8
- Ecclesiastes 1:2
- Ecclesiastes 2:11
- 2 Thessalonians 2:11
- Genesis 1:26
- Isaiah 61:1-11

## The Prayer:

"How precious Your thoughts towards me, O God, how great the sum of them is! Father, You bless those who reverence Your name and delight in Your commands.

In the midst of my most inner toil moils and outer conflicts, I will not be moved. For my heart remains steadfast, trusting in You and your overall plan for my life.

I will remain faithful and I will stay firmly grounded as I overcome my daily obstacles. Help me to learn in my hardships the valuable lessons along the way, as I press toward the goal which You have called me.

Thank You for showing me that the only value I have is in You and that You will give me beauty for ashes, the oil of joy for mourning, the garment of praise for the spirit of heaviness; that I can be called a tree of righteousness, the planting of the Lord, that You may be glorified. In Jesus' name. Amen."

CPSIA information can be obtained at www.ICGtesting.com
Printed in the USA
BVOW08s1314210816

459645BV00001B/3/P